PRAISE FOR JONATHAN SCHELL

THE FATE OF THE EARTH
"The most important book of the decade, perhaps of the century."
—Harrison E. Salisbury

"There have been thousands of commentaries on what this new destructive power of man means; but my guess is that Schell's book . . . will become the classic statement of the emerging consciousness." —Max Lerner, *New Republic*

THE TIME OF ILLUSION
"By persuasively connecting the Nixon years to the larger dilemmas of our time, Mr. Schell has elevated a shabby political story to the level of tragedy. And one closes his deeply intelligent book not with feelings of vindication or outrage, but with a sense of understanding and equanimity that only tragedy can evoke."
—Christopher Lehmann-Haupt, *The New York Time*s

"A thoughtful and deservedly acclaimed meditation on the decade which, in 1974, 'finally brought the American Constitutional system to the edge of breakdown.'" —*Foreign Affairs*

THE UNCONQUERABLE WORLD
"Schell, in this profoundly important book, wants us to being thinking about how we can use democracy—the actions of people, rather than governments—to bring about a peaceful world." —Howard Zinn, *The Boston Globe*

"*The Unconquerable World* is Mr. Schell's most ambitious, and over time will be regarded as his most significant work. . . . The book mounts perhaps the most impressive argument ever made that there exists a viable and desirable alternative to a continued reliance on war and that the failure to seize this opportunity will bring catastrophic results to America and the world."
—Richard Falk, *The New York Times*

"Wise, passionate, eloquent, and infused with historical vision rare in these dark times, Jonathan Schell's new book makes a powerful case for the realism of idealism in breaking the cycles of violence that threaten to destroy us all."
—John Dower, Pulitzer Prize-winning author of *Embracing Defeat*

A HOLE IN THE WORLD

An Unfolding Story of War, Protest
and the New American Order

Jonathan Schell

NATION BOOKS *New York*

A HOLE IN THE WORLD: *An Unfolding Story of War, Protest
and the New American Order*

Copyright © 2004 Jonathan Schell

Published by
Nation Books
An Imprint of Avalon Publishing Group
245 West 17th St., 11th Floor
New York, NY 10011

Nation Books is a co-publishing venture of the Nation Institute and Avalon
Publishing Group Incorporated.

These essays originally appeared in *The Nation* and are being kindly reprinted with
the permission of *The Nation*. Copyright © *The Nation*. All rights reserved. "Politics in
Command" and "America's Vulnerable Imperialism" appeared in YaleGlobal Online,
(*http://yaleglobal.yale.edu*) a publication of the Yale Center for the Study of Globalization, and are reprinted by permission. Copyright © 2004 Yale Center for the Study of
Globalization.

Library of Congress Cataloging-in-Publication Data is available.

ISBN 1-56025-600-1

9 8 7 6 5 4 3 2 1

Book design by Simon M. Sullivan

Printed in the United States of America
Distributed by Publishers Group West

For Hamilton Fish, President of The Nation Institute, and, for half a decade now, great and inspired sustainer of our common work and great friend

Introduction:
A Story in Real Time

JONATHAN SCHELL

A FEW DAYS after the attacks of September 11, I began to write a series of columns for *The Nation* magazine. History, as everyone realized almost immediately, had been jolted onto a new path. It seemed to me that the consequences of that day, whatever they turned out to be, were bound to constitute a sort of single story. The idea of the column was to tell that story and reflect on it as it unfolded. This book is the result. Almost immediately after the attack, people began to call the site of the missing World Trade Center, six blocks south of where I lived, Ground Zero—a designation that of course evoked the ground zero of nuclear annihilation. The communal instinct for naming things struck me as having been unerring in this instance. Sooner or later, I believed, the story was bound to circle back to the reality of nuclear danger; and so, at the suggestion of my son Matthew, I called the new column "Letter from Ground Zero", meaning to capture the old as well as the new meaning of the term.

That hunch was borne out, yet most of what was about to

happen was unguessable. Who would have thought that, in the months to come, the president would announce, in the name of nonproliferation, a whole series of possible wars; that in the name of this policy he would overthrow the government of Iraq; that he would adopt a doctrine of nothing less than global American hegemony by means of the unilateral use of force; that protests opposing the war would break out all over the world; that the weapons the war was fought to find in Iraq would not be there; that in the meantime North Korea would become a nuclear power and America's ally Pakistan would sell nuclear-weapons components all over the world; that a rebellion against the new American foreign policy (among others) would transform the Democratic Party into an angry mass with a real chance of beating the president in the 2004 election?

Yet what now interests me as much as the things that happened are the things that faded away—the sprouts that never grew, the doors that wouldn't open, the baseless hopes, the unwarranted alarms, the characters that loomed large for a second and then disappeared, the theories that didn't pan out, the dashed plans, the many, many paths not taken—paths examined carefully at the time but then forgotten forever. Looking over these pages, I notice Mohammed Zahir Shaw, putative future king of Afghanistan, over whom much ink was spilled; the adventurer Mohammed Mohsen Zubaidi, who, in the power vacuum of immediate post-war Baghdad, left faint fingerprints on history by briefly claiming to be mayor of the city; General Jay Garner, the American proconsul in Iraq who lasted just three weeks on the job.

Hannah Arendt liked to quote a saying of Henri Proudhon: "The fecundity of events greatly exceeds the prudence of the statesman." And of columnists, we can readily add. The historian, writing after the fact, has the inestimable advantage of knowing the end of the story before writing the first word. The contemporary, on the other hand, is like a miner seeking his way in the dark with a dim lantern, able to see only a few steps ahead, if that. There is little opportunity here for the grand overview, the master idea that seems to make sense of it all, the key that unlocks history's secrets. No matter how many cell phones, satellites, global linkups, the "communications industry" may now have, the ability to know what will happen tomorrow does not improve. Foretelling the future is one field in which progress has been nil.

People speak of the "march of history," but the expression is an illusion of hindsight. History does not march; more likely it creeps for a while, then suddenly dashes ahead, then hides again, then sneaks along by a hidden detour, then springs some inconceivable surprise on an unready world.

History-writing tends to reinforce a feeling of inevitability: things had to be as they were. As readers of history, we feel satisfied if we are given "causes" that seem to have produced "effects." The weight of what actually was cancels out the reality of what might have been. Story-telling in real time, on the other hand, offers a different portrait of events: at each point, a veil is drawn across the future, the path forward is unknown, many futures are possible, decisions lie open, and what they finally are matters desperately. What might be remains, incurably, as vivid as what will be.

If chronicles in real time lack the settled lessons and wisdom that seem possible in the writing of history, they can, at their best, capture the unfixed, unknown, anxiety-ridden, reality of life in the moment—a wisdom, if you want to call it that, not of knowing but of not-knowing. It isn't found in hindsight but on the cusp of every moment, as it unfolds.

NEW YORK
MARCH, 2004

A Hole in the World

ON TUESDAY MORNING, a piece was torn out of our world. A patch of blue sky that should not have been there opened up in the New York skyline. In my neighborhood—I live six blocks from the World Trade Center—the heavens were raining human beings. Our city was changed forever. Our country was changed forever. Our world was changed forever.

It will take months merely to know what happened, far longer to feel so much grief, longer still to understand its meaning. It's already clear, however, that one aspect of the catastrophe is of supreme importance for the future: the danger of the use of weapons of mass destruction, and especially the use of nuclear weapons. This danger includes their use by a terrorist group but is by no means restricted to it. It is part of a larger danger that has been for the most part ignored since the end of the Cold War.

Among the small number who have been concerned with nuclear arms in recent years—they have pretty much all known one another by their first names—it was commonly heard that the world would not return its attention to this subject until a nuclear weapon was again set off somewhere in the world. *Then,* the tiny club said to itself, the world would awaken to its danger. Many of the ingredients of the catastrophe were obvious. The repeated suicide-homicides of the bombers in Israel made it obvious that there were people so possessed by their cause that, in an exaltation of hatred, they would do anything in its name. Many reports—most recently an article in the *New York Times* on the very morning of the attack—reminded the public that the world was awash in nuclear materials and the wherewithal for other weapons of mass destruction. Russia is bursting at the seams with these materials. The suicide bombers and the market in nuclear materials was that two-plus-two that points toward the proverbial necessary four. But history is a trickster. The fates came up with a horror that was unforeseen. No one had identified the civilian airliner as a weapon of mass destruction, but it occurred to the diabolical imagination of those who conceived Tuesday's attack that it could be one. The invention illumined the nature of terrorism in modern times. These terrorists carried no bombs—only knives, if initial reports are to be believed. In short, they turned the tremendous forces inherent in modern technical society—in this case, Boeing 767s brimming with jet fuel—against itself.

So it is also with the more commonly recognized weapons of mass destruction. Their materials can be built the hard way, from scratch, as Iraq came within an ace of doing until stopped by the Gulf War and as Pakistan and India have done, or they can be diverted from Russian, or for that matter American or English or French or Chinese, stockpiles. In the one case, it is nuclear know-how that is turned against its inventors, in the other it is their hardware. Either way, it is "blowback"—the use of a technical capacity against its creator—and, as such, represents the pronounced suicidal tendencies of modern society.

This suicidal bent—nicely captured in the name of the still current nuclear policy "mutual assured destruction"—of course exists in forms even more devastating than possible terrorist attacks. India and Pakistan, which both possess nuclear weapons and have recently engaged in one of their many hot wars, are the likeliest candidates. Most important—and most forgotten—are the some 30,000 nuclear weapons that remain in the arsenals of Russia and the United States. The Bush Administration has announced its intention of breaking out of the antiballistic missile treaty of 1972, which bans antinuclear defenses, and the Russians have answered that if this treaty is abandoned the whole framework of nuclear arms control built up over thirty years may collapse. There is no quarrel between the United States and Russia that suggests a nuclear exchange between them, but accidents are another matter, and, as Tuesday's attack has shown, the mood and even the structure of the international order can change overnight.

What should be done? Should the terrorists who carried out Tuesday's attacks be brought to justice and punished, as the President wants to do? Of course. Who should be punished if not people who would hurl a cargo of innocent human beings against a fixed target of other innocent human beings? (When weighing the efficiency—as distinct from the satisfaction—of punishment, however, it is well to remember that the immediate attackers have administered the supposed supreme punishment of death to themselves.) Should further steps be taken to protect the country and the world from terrorism, including nuclear terrorism? They should. And yet even as we do these things, we must hold, as if to life itself, to a fundamental truth that has been known to all thoughtful people since the destruction of Hiroshima: *There is no technical solution to the vulnerability of modern populations to weapons of mass destruction.* After the attack, Secretary of Defense Rumsfeld placed US forces on the highest state of alert and ordered destroyers and aircraft carriers to take up positions up and down the coasts of the United States. But none of these measures can repeal the vulnerability of modern society to its own inventions, revealed by that heartbreaking gap in the New York skyline. This, obviously, holds equally true for that other Maginot line, the proposed system of national missile defense. Thirty billion dollars is being spent on intelligence annually. We can assume that some portion of that was devoted to protecting the World Trade Center after it was first bombed in 1993. There may have been mistakes—maybe we'll find out—but the truth is that no one on earth can demonstrate that the expenditure of even ten times that amount can prevent a terrorist attack on the United States or any other country. The combination of the extraordinary power of modern technology, the universal and instantaneous spread of information in the information age, and the mobility inherent in a globalized economy prevents it.

Man, however, is not merely a technical animal. Aristotle pointed out that we are also a political animal, and it is to politics that we must return for the solutions that hold promise. That means returning to the treaties that the United States has recently been discarding like so much old newspaper—the one dealing, for example, with an International Criminal Court (useful for tracking down terrorists and bringing them to justice), with global warming and, above all, of course, with nuclear arms and the other weapons of mass destruction, biological and chemical. The United States and seven other countries now rely for their national security on the retaliatory execution of destruction a millionfold greater than the Tuesday attacks. The exit from this folly, by which we endanger ourselves as much as others, must be found. Rediscovering ourselves as political animals also means understanding the sources of the hatred that the United States has incurred in a decade of neglect and, worse, neglect of international affairs—a task that is highly unwelcome to many in current circumstances but nevertheless is indispensable to the future safety of the United States and the world.

It would be disrespectful of the dead to in any way minimize the catastrophe that has overtaken New York. Yet at the same time we must keep room in our minds for the fact that it could have been worse. To lose two huge buildings and the people in them is one thing; to lose all of Manhattan—or much, much more—is another. The emptiness in the sky can spread. We have been warned.

A Sense of Proportion

OCTOBER 8, 2001

THE BLOW AGAINST the United States has landed. As we go
to press, the counterblow is awaited. Those deciding what it will
be face a devilish conundrum. A great injury seems to call for a
great response—a "response commensurate to the horror," in
the words of Cokie Roberts of ABC News. Unfortunately for
the satisfaction of this impulse, a proportional antagonist is not
always available. It is a perplexing but inescapable fact of our
time that great crimes can be committed by puny forces. The
obvious example is assassination—an experience branded in
American memory by the assassination of President John
Kennedy. The gigantic shock of that event seemed to require a
gigantic explanation. The mind recoiled at the idea that a single
anonymous person could affect the lives of so many so deeply.
Many found their satisfaction in conspiracy theories. The government of the day, however, felt it had to resist these tempta-
tions. It was the office of the Warren Commission to tidy up the
affair, even at the cost of many overlooked suggestive facts,
many unpursued leads. During the Cold War, the stakes were

judged too high to indulge in endless investigations that might undermine the already tense relations of the two hostile superpowers, ready and able to blow each other up in half an hour.

September 11 also presents a maddening disproportion between cause and effect. To be sure, the assault was not the act of an individual; yet at most a few score were directly involved. Behind them—if current speculation is correct—might be a few hundred potential coconspirators; and behind them, perhaps, some thousands of active supporters. These forces present a dim, vague target. A direct, immediate response against them cannot possibly be "commensurate" with the horror—not only because they are few but because they are dispersed and hidden. That has left the Administration searching for larger targets, and it appears to believe it has found them in its determination to, in George W. Bush's words, "make no distinction between the terrorists who committed these acts and those who harbor them." The deliberate erasure of the distinction between perpetrators and supporters obviously has opened the way to an attack on one or more states—targets that, whatever their level of responsibility, would indeed be commensurate in size with the horror. It was in pursuit of such a target, of course, that the United States in effect dispatched a team of Pakistanis to the Taliban government of Afghanistan to persuade it to yield up its "guest" Osama bin Laden, who is suspected of masterminding the attack.

The Taliban have indeed sheltered bin Laden, and an effort to end that support makes sense. However, a military strike against the Taliban or any other regime is full of perils that—hard as it is to imagine in the wake of the recent tragedy—are far greater than the dangers we already face. Civilian casualties, even in retaliation, stir indignation, as we now know so deeply. Anger is the best recruiter for violent causes, including radical Islam. There is a distinct danger of self-fulfilling prophecy. By striking indiscriminately we can create the "commensurate" antagonist that we now lack. The danger takes many forms. In the first place, moderate Muslims who now dislike US policy toward their countries but who also oppose terror may begin to support it. In the second place, by attacking radical regimes we may undermine other, conservative regimes. One is the repressive, monarchical regime of Saudi Arabia, possessor of the world's oil supplies. Another is Pakistan. Its leader, Gen. Pervez Musharraf, is a military dictator with a tenuous grip on power. His most powerful opponents are not the democrats he overthrew in his military coup but Islamic militants, who honeycomb his army and could, if angered enough by the humiliation of his regime by demands from the United States, possibly overthrow it. Pakistan, of course, has been a nuclear power since May 1998. Will the United States, in its fury at a terrible attack that was, nevertheless, on the "conventional" scale, create a fresh nuclear danger to itself and the world?

It's rightly said that in the face of the attack, America must be strong. Its military strength is beyond doubt, but strength consists of more than firepower. The strength now needed is the discipline of restraint. Restraint does not mean inaction; it means patience, discrimination, action in concert with other nations, resolve over the long haul. We live, as we have since 1945, in an age of weapons of mass destruction—nuclear, chemical, and biological. During the Cold War there was one ladder of escalation that led to oblivion. Now there are many. Now as then, escalation is "unthinkable." It must be avoided at all cost.

The Power of the Powerful

OF COURSE THERE can be no such thing as a literal letter from ground zero—neither from the ground zeros of September 11 nor from the potential nuclear ground zero that is the origin of the expression. There are no letters from the beyond. (By now, "zero" has the double meaning of zero distance from the bombardier's assigned coordinates and the nothingness that's left when his work is done.) As it happens, though, I live six blocks from the ruins of the north tower of the World Trade Center, which is about as close as you can be to ground zero without having been silenced. My specific neighborhood was violated, mutilated. As I write these words, the acrid, dank, rancid stink—it is the smell of death—of the still-smoking site is in my nostrils. Not that these things confer any great distinction—they are merely the local embodiment of the circumstance, felt more or less keenly by everyone in the world in the aftermath of the attack, that in our age of weapons of mass destruction every square foot of our globe can become such a ground zero in a twinkling. We have long known this intellectually, but now we know it viscerally, as a nausea in the pit of the stomach that is unlikely to go away. What to do to change this condition, it seems to me, is the most important of the practical tasks that the crisis requires us to perform.

It takes time for the human reality of the losses to sink in. The eye is quick but the heart is slow. I had two experiences this week that helped me along. It occurred to me that I would be a very bad journalist and maybe a worse neighbor if, living just a few blocks from the catastrophe, I did not manage to get through the various checkpoints to visit the site. A press pass was useless; it got me no closer than my own home. A hole in the storm-fence circling the site worked better. I found myself in the midst of a huge peaceable army of helpers in a thousand uniforms—military and civilian. I was somehow unprepared by television for what I saw when I arrived at ground zero. Television had seemed to show mostly a low hillock of rubble from which the famous bucket brigade of rescuers was passing out pieces of debris. This proved to be a keyhole vision of the site. In fact, it was a gigantic, varied, panoramic landscape of destruction, an Alps of concrete, plastic, and twisted metal, rising tier upon tier in the smoky distance. Around the perimeter and in the surrounding streets, a cornucopia of food, drinks (thousands of crates of spring water, Gatorade, etc.) and other provisions contributed by well-wishers from around the country was heaped up, as if some main of consumer goods on its way to the Trade Center had burst and disgorged its flood upon the sidewalks. The surrounding buildings, smashed but still standing, looked down eyelessly on their pulverized brethren. The pieces of the facade of the towers that are often shown in photographs—gigantic forks, or bent spatulas—loomed surprisingly high over the scene with dread majesty. Entry into the ruins by the rescue workers was being accomplished by a cage, or gondola, suspended by a crane, as if in some infernal ski resort. When I arrived at the southern rim, the rescuers were all standing silent watching one of these cages being lifted out of the ruins. Shortly, a small pile of something not shaped like a human being but covered by an American flag was brought out in an open buggy. It was the remains, a solemn nurse told me, of one of the firemen who had given his life for the people in the building. And then the slow work began again. Although the site was more terrible even than I had imagined, seeing was somehow reassuring. Unvisited, the site, so near my home, had preyed on my imagination.

A few days later—one week after the catastrophe—I took my dog for a walk in the evening in Riverside Park, on the upper West Side. Soft orange clouds drifted over the Hudson River and the New Jersey shore. In the dim, cavernous green of the park, normal things were occurring—people were out for walks or jogging, children were playing in a playground. To the south, a slender moon hung in the sky. I found myself experiencing an instant of surprise: So it was still there! It had not dropped out of the sky. That was good. After all, our local southern mountain peaks—the twin towers—had fallen. The world seemed to steady around the surviving moon. "Peace" became more than a word. It was the world of difference between the bottom half of Manhattan and the top. It was the persistence of all the wonderful, ordinary things before my eyes.

Curiously, it was only after this moment of return to confidence in the continuity of life that the shape and size of the change that had been wrought in the world a week before began to come into view. The very immensity of that change—and, what was something different, the news coverage of that change—was itself a prime fact of the new situation. In an instant and without warning on a fine fall morning, the known world had been jerked aside like a mere slide in a projector, and a new world had been rammed into its place. I have before me the *New York Times* of September 11, which went to press, of course, the night before the attack. It is news from Atlantis. "Key Leaders," were talking of "Possible Deals to Revive Economy," a headline said, but who was paying attention now? Were "School Dress Codes" still in a struggle with "A Sea of Bare Flesh"? Yes, but it was hard to give the matter much thought. Was "Morning TV" still a "Hot Market" in "a Nation of Early Risers"? It was, but not for the reasons given in the article. Only one headline—"Nuclear Booty: More Smugglers Use Asia Route"—seemed fit for the day's events.

Has the eye of the world ever shifted more abruptly or completely than it did on September 11? The destruction of Hiroshima of course comes to mind. It, too, was prepared in secrecy and fell like a thunderbolt upon the world. But it came after years of a world war and ended the war, whereas the September 11 attack came in a time of peace and—so our President has said—started a war. The assassination of Archduke Ferdinand on June 28, 1914, starting the First World War, is another candidate. Yet the possibility of war among the great powers had long been discussed, and many previous crises—in the Far East, in the Mediterranean, in the Balkans—had threatened war. It was not the event but the aftermath (we are still living in it)— the war's ferocity and duration and the war-born horrors that sprang out of it to afflict the entire twentieth century—that changed the world. Also, whereas the guns of August touched off a chain of events—the invocation of a web of treaty agreements, the predetermined mobilization schedules of great armies—that statesmanship and diplomacy seemed powerless to prevent, today little seems predetermined, and the latitude of choice, ranging from international police work to multifront major war, seems exceptionally wide.

All the more important, then, is the character and depth of the first public reaction. Today, when it comes to reactions in general, there is a new structural factor of the first importance to keep in mind. This, of course, is the news media, whose very nature it seems to be to magnify stories. These stories can, like coverage of the Gary Condit drama, be trivial and ridiculous or, like the Monica Lewinsky scandal, half serious and half ridiculous, or, like the September 11 attack, wholly serious. There are many hundreds of thousands of journalists in the world today. I think of them—us—as a kind of army, indeed, a very large one, as armies go. It is an army that terrorists almost always seek to recruit. Their deeds seek to influence public opinion, which is to say public will. The terrorist act of September 11, though costing more lives than any other, was no exception. As so many have observed, it was, probably by evil design, a disaster film— even a comic book or video game—brought sickeningly to life: horrific "infotainment" or "reality TV." The use of real life and real lives to enact a plot lifted out of the trashiest entertainments was an element of the peculiar debasement of the event. (The terrorist's use of the disaster genre has of course left Hollywood groping for some new stock-in-trade to amuse us with.)

The media army has thus been faced with an old dilemma on a new scale: If it carried out its responsibility of covering the news, it at the same time risked advancing the agenda of the terrorists. Of course, the terrorists can miscalculate the consequences of recruiting the media army. If the hijackers' hope on the 11th was to weaken the will of the United States to oppose their cause, obviously their plan backfired. American will to defeat them could scarcely be stronger. On the other hand, weakening American will to lash out may not have been their goal. Just the contrary may be the case. If I were a terrorist leader, there is nothing I would be praying for more ardently than an attack by the United States on one or more Islamic countries leading to the death of many innocent Muslims. If this happened, then, having successfully recruited the media army, I would have recruited the armed forces of the United States as well and would be well on my way to creating the war between America and Islamic civilization that at present I could only dream of.

Last week, it looked as if the United States might fall into this trap. Of course it was not media saturation alone that created the possibility. The wish to retaliate on the scale of the injury, an ageless instinct, would have been running powerfully in the country in any case. In his speech before the joint session of Congress, President Bush issued an ultimatum that the Taliban government of Afghanistan was bound to reject (and did reject): It must, among other things, deliver up its "guest" Osama bin Laden and all other terrorists in Afghanistan to American justice, and open its country to full inspection. If the Taliban refused, Bush said, they would "share the fate of the terrorists." Here was a clear declaration, if there ever was one, of an intention to overthrow a government.

By this week, however, there were signs that the effects of the President's high-proof rhetoric, which press and public alike gulped down eagerly, were wearing off, and greater sobriety was setting in. Secretary of Defense Donald Rumsfeld, reported to belong to a hawkish faction in the Administration, eager to topple not only the Taliban but also the regime of President Saddam Hussein of Iraq, was surprisingly asking, "Is it likely that an aircraft carrier or a cruise missile is going to find a person?" He thought not, and suggested instead that "this is going to happen over a sustained period of time because of a broadly based effort where bank accounts are frozen, where pieces of intelligence are provided." As for Afghanistan, it was "not as though there is a front, and that there are good guys and bad guys," he surprisingly opined. In the clearest indication of a reversal of course, President Bush himself said, "We're not into nation-building." Countries that aren't into nation-building are ill advised to get into nation-toppling. However, American forces continued to pour into the Middle East, and the Administration could at any time switch back to a war policy.

Among the public, too, there were signs of cooling fever, if not of lessening resolve. Atlantis—the world of happenings other than those of September 11—began to poke above the waves. Among the recommendations that the Red Cross made for dealing psychologically with national crises was to avoid watching the news all the time. This is sound advice—as good for national policy as for mental well-being. A will to do justice that burns with a steady, low flame will be more useful than one that flares up all at once and then gutters out.

Vaclav Havel once invoked the "power of the powerless," by

which he meant the power of the nonviolent weak to defy and defeat totalitarian regimes through unarmed acts of noncooperation and defiance. But the powerful have some power, too. Terrorism is jujitsu, by which the violent weak use the power of the powerful to overthrow them. Nineteen men with plastic knives and box cutters (so far, investigators have been unable to identify a larger network that supported the act) used some of the United States' biggest and most sophisticated aircraft to knock down some of its biggest buildings, all in the apparent hope of enlisting the world's media army to provoke America's real army to commit acts that would rally opinion in the terrorists' part of the world to their own side. But the powerful can refuse to cooperate. Tom Friedman of the *Times* advised that the United States, like the Taliban, should act "a *little bit crazy*." But the Taliban are a poor model. That way lies our undoing. When all is said and done, it is not in the power of America's enemies to defeat us. Only we can do that. We should refrain.

The Phony War

ON SEPTEMBER 1, 1939, Hitler's armies rolled across the western border of Poland. On September 3, England and France declared war on Germany. But the two great powers, unable to intervene in strength in Poland, did not take action right away. A lull—"prolonged and oppressive," in Churchill's words—followed. The "phony war," as many called it, had begun. (Churchill called it the "twilight war.") England promptly sent bombers over Germany—but only to drop millions of propaganda leaflets. And so the time was also called "the confetti war." Everyone knew, however, that the die had been cast, that real war would come. And it did come, of course, at a cost of some forty-six million lives.

On September 20, 2001, war was once again declared—this time by an American President, supported by Congress. But once again there was a lull, a kind of phony war. The President's words before the joint session of Congress were clear enough. Either the Taliban government of Afghanistan must yield up the Islamic extremist Osama bin Laden and other accused terrorists or it would "share in their fate." And yet over the next several days, in perhaps the swiftest climb-down from an ultimatum in American history, this clear commitment appeared to melt away. It was a welcome change to dovish analysts, but vexing to hawks and confusing to all. Did the United States really mean to unseat the Taliban? The President's spokesman, Ari Fleischer, didn't see it that way. When Bush, using much politer language than he had before Congress, suggested that the best way to bring to justice those responsible for the September 11 terrorist attacks was "to ask for the cooperation of citizens within Afghanistan who may be tired of having the Taliban in place," Fleischer rushed out to assure the world that American action "is not designed to replace one regime with another regime." Two days after the attack, Deputy Secretary of Defense Paul Wolfowitz said that US policy should be "ending states who sponsor terrorism," but four days after that Secretary of State Colin Powell said he'd prefer to say that "ending terrorism is where I would like to leave it and let Mr. Wolfowitz speak for himself." At the end of September, Wolfowitz himself said, "I think it can't be stressed enough that everybody who is waiting for military action . . . needs to rethink this thing." It was as if, after their declaration of war on Germany in 1939, France and England had announced the next week that they hadn't exactly meant Germany, maybe hadn't even meant war. Had the President been bluffing? After reflection, was he moving to a more sober policy, without being able to say so?

At the beginning of October, the winds seemed to shift again. Britain's Prime Minister, Tony Blair, declared that the Taliban's choice was "to surrender the terrorists or surrender power," and

Bush said that this had been "exactly" his message to Congress. Bush had said that the United States was not "into nation-building," but now an eighty-six-year-old former Afghan monarch, Mohammed Zahir Shah, was rolled forward as the possible leader of a regime to replace the Taliban. Government counsel to the American public was as changeable as policy. Ari Fleischer wanted Americans to get on with a "normal" existence, and President Bush wanted them to "get on board" airplanes again, but Attorney General John Ashcroft warned, "We think that there is a very serious threat of additional problems now," and added, "and, frankly, as the United States responds, that threat may escalate."

The confusion was deeper still. In 1939, England and France did not know when war would come or what form it would take, but they knew without doubt that they were at war, and, what is more important, they knew what a war was. In the phony war of 2001, there was no agreement on either point. Many observers agreed with the *Times*'s Tom Friedman that "the equivalent of World War III" was upon us. But was this true? Are we embarked on a path of horror equivalent to—or greater than—that taken by the world after 1914 and 1939? That was the question that, above all others, has hung terrifyingly in the air in this grief-stricken, nervous, uncertain interval between the injury to the United States and the response, between the attack and the counterattack.

It was not easy to answer. On the one hand, the world of 2001 did not present an array of great hostile powers, ready to wage total war on one another, as the world of 1939 had done. The United States was indeed such a power, but its immediate attackers had been a force of nineteen men armed with box cutters. Years of battle among great alliances of nations was not in the cards. On the other hand, as the attack had shown, the world of 2001 was stocked with technical instruments of destruction that enabled a very few people, or a feeble state, to wreak almost incalculable devastation. It was with good reason that the United States was awakening in shock to the danger of attacks with weapons of mass destruction. In "hot pursuit" (as Bush put it) of the terrorists, the United States had already seriously destabilized one weak yet nuclear-armed power: Pakistan. If Islamist extremists took over that nation, would the United States launch a preemptive strike against its nuclear arsenal? If it did, would it succeed, and would the extremist government, or its terrorist allies, find a way to retaliate upon American soil? Would someone else? After September 11, do we still imagine that we are invulnerable?

Some voices were calling for major conventional war. The columnist Charles Krauthammer demanded that the United States overthrow the governments of four countries: Afghanistan, Iraq, Syria, and Iran. According to some news reports, there was support in the Administration for such a program. If a campaign on this scale is launched, the prediction that World War III is upon us will become more likely. Is the world of 2001 set on a course that will cost tens of millions of lives, or more? The men with the box cutters cannot by themselves bring it off. But an enraged, blind superpower could manage it. Krauthammer's four wars could do it. They could transform the local catastrophe in New York and Washington into a global one. Yet it remains equally true that a wise, restrained superpower can head off such a fate. Which will it be? The attack of September 11 did not decide. What the United States does now will decide.

Annihilation and
the Ways of Peace

OCTOBER 29, 2001

ONE MONTH AFTER September 11, ground zero—six blocks
from where I live—remains unquiet. Inextinguishable subter-
ranean fires belch smoke into the neighborhood, as if the ruin
were an active volcano, spreading a stench whose source we do
not care to think about. The global crisis set in motion by the
attack has been active, too. In its fourth week, two major erup-
tions occurred: the beginning of the Anglo-American war on
Afghanistan and the outbreak of anthrax in Florida. The latter
could turn out to be the more important of the two. Robert
Stevens, a photo editor at *The Sun,* a tabloid paper given to
attacking Osama bin Laden in colorful headlines, died of the ill-
ness, and a coworker was exposed. The FBI has made the Sun
building a crime scene, and experts on anthrax are at a loss to
imagine any way that the outbreak can be attributed to natural
causes. If the worst fears are borne out—that the terrorists who
carried out the September 11 attacks were responsible—then the

world will have crossed a dread verge. Weapons of mass destruction—though perhaps used in this instance in sniper fashion to kill only a few—will have been introduced into the conflict. I of course do not wish to suggest that it is unimportant whether these fears are based on fact or not. But everyone knows that the danger that such weapons will be used is the greatest of those inherent in the situation, and the world will make no mistake if it turns out that a false alarm has inspired it to act to protect itself. We might even count ourselves fortunate that we were prompted to respond by an event that was either nonexistent or on a small scale. Action taken under conditions of mass attack is unlikely to be as rational or as carefully considered.

The two events were reflected in the divided mood of the American public. On the one hand, public support for the war was strong. On the other hand, a profound, unmistakable unease was palpable in the land. Fear of weapons of mass destruction was part of it. A sheriff in the small town of Pendleton, Oregon, told a *New York Times* reporter, "What I realize now for the first time is that we can be big and bad and still be got." But fear was not the only note struck. There were expressions of worry that the Afghans would now suffer what Americans—not used to this sort of thing—had suffered. While the public found the assault in Afghanistan "inescapable and just," the *Washington Post* reported, "the jingoistic call for annihilation was heard less often than the hope that the death of innocents might be kept to a minimum." There were signs that awareness of a common peril had created a feeling of common humanity.

The two currents of reaction have in fact been present since the very first second of the crisis. When the attacks occurred, the thought that flashed spontaneously into millions of minds was that our world had changed forever. But what, exactly, was the change that everyone felt, and why did awareness of it come so quickly? It was, I suggest, an immediate, bone-deep recognition of the utter perishability of all human works and all human beings in the face of human destructive powers. The change was felt immediately because it was the recognition of something already known, if rarely thought about—known since 1945, when Hiroshima was destroyed by an atomic bomb. The twin towers of the World Trade Center were the most massive objects in the City of New York, perhaps in all America. If, without any warning, they could evaporate in the blink of eye, what was safe?

The peril of further terrorist attacks was of course uppermost in people's thoughts, but in the background were the still existing, though strangely missionless, nuclear arsenals currently in the hands of eight nations. These, too, soon obtruded onto the scene. The conceivable overthrow of the military dictatorship in Pakistan by extreme Muslim forces angry that their nation had been coerced by the United States into a supporting role in the attack on Afghanistan raised the specter that Pakistan's nuclear weapons might fall into the hands of a Taliban-like regime. Here in the United States, Billy Graham's son, the Rev. Franklin Graham, called for their use against America's enemies. Defense Secretary Donald Rumsfeld, asked whether the United States was contemplating the use of nuclear weapons, twice declined to rule it out. On the second occasion, he even upped the ante, pointing out that during the Cold War the United States had refused to rule out the "first use" of nuclear weapons. That is still US policy, notably in the event of the use of chemical or biological weapons.

The destruction of the twin towers, in short, was a taste of annihilation, a small piece of the end of the world. Recognition of this—let us call it the annihilation model of the shape of the crisis—educated, you might say, the viscera of the public. In the public's conscious mind, on the other hand, another model prevailed, which can be called the war model. In this model, which formed the basis for President George W. Bush's speech before the joint session of Congress, September 11 was Pearl Harbor and the starting gun for a long military conflict—"America's New War," as CNN had it. However, even the Administration soon had to recognize that the war model fit the actual situation imperfectly, at best. The death of 5,000 certainly created moral and legal justification enough for waging war. The right of self-defense is clearly recognized in international law. But not every action that is justifiable is wise. Who, in this picture, was the equivalent of Japan or Nazi Germany? Where were the targets? How were they to be hit? What could be the role of armed forces in fighting against terrorism, in which police forces have traditionally been used? (When the town of Omagh was bombed in 1998, killing twenty-nine people, Britain did not shower Northern Ireland with cruise missiles.) And in fact, in the weeks between the President's warlike speech and the launch of the attacks, the Administration backpedaled significantly from the war model. Rumsfeld's definition of US war aims was remarkably modest and vague. It was to "create conditions for sustained antiterrorist action and humanitarian relief." Would ground troops be sent in? Would they occupy

Afghanistan? Would the Taliban be overthrown? Would the Northern Alliance be installed to replace them, or perhaps the former King of Afghanistan, Mohammed Zahir Shah? If installed, would either of these seek to "root out" terrorists? Would they succeed? When it was all over, would the number of terrorists be greater or fewer than before? Even if US forces won the war in Afghanistan (no easy task) would it lose the war on terrorism? Military strategy faded into the mist of these unanswered political questions.

If the annihilation model had been the basis for understanding the crisis, policies of a very different character would have been adopted. The dangers of escalation—of heightened fervor in the Islamic world, of tit-for-tat strikes between Islamic forces and American troops—would have been uppermost in official minds. Military restraint then would have been the order of the day from the very beginning of the effort rather than being introduced as an afterthought. War would have been seen as a sort of self-indulgence. Political considerations—the mood and response of the world's one billion Muslims, for instance—would now be dominating. The fight against terrorism would take the form of police action, conducted by the international coalition so painstakingly put together by Secretary of State Colin Powell. Military action would play a merely supporting role—in the form, perhaps, of the occasional commando raid to seize or destroy a terrorist cell when its location could be ascertained by intelligence. The model for military action, insofar as it occurred, would not be today's blitzkrieg but a siege.

The distinction between waging war and preventing annihilation is not a new one. The military policies of the entire Cold

War were based on it. Preventing annihilation was the foremost stated goal of the principal strategy of the age, the doctrine of nuclear deterrence. Policy-makers were keenly aware that actual fighting must be resisted because it could lead to oblivion for all concerned. Now the danger of annihilation has reared its head again, and once again the perils of escalation are before us. The restraint that was slowly learned in the Cold War has to be relearned in this new context. This time, however, deterrence can hardly serve. Terrorists have no countries to hold hostage to retaliatory nuclear destruction. They possess only their lives, and these they throw away with their own hands.

New policies to address the new danger of annihilation are needed, and these originate far from the precincts of war. One is a comprehensive global effort to rid the world of weapons of mass destruction—a plan in which a readiness of the great powers to disarm would lay the foundation for unchallengeable policies of nonproliferation, which in turn would lay the basis for the tightest possible international control of these weapons' special materials and technologies. No plan can reduce the danger by 100 percent, but an 80 or 90 percent reduction of risk should be possible. Another, even vaster and more difficult undertaking is a systematic campaign to damp down and then politically resolve the world's festering local conflicts, starting with those in the Middle East. Such steps have always been desirable. Now they have become essential for survival.

Can such sweeping, positive ambitions have any bearing at this hour, which has turned out, for the time being, to be one of war? British Prime Minister Tony Blair, for one, thinks they can. In his speech to the recent Labour Party conference, he proposed a "politics of globalization" to complement the economics of globalization. He called for the international community to address with new resolve the conflicts in Rwanda, in Israel and Palestine, and in Ireland, among others; for action to redress the growing global gap between rich and poor; for measures to remedy global warming and other environmental ills. These were not original ideas, but to set them forth at this moment was original. Blair deserves credit merely for striking this hopeful note at a time of such foreboding. However, Blair located his vision on the far shore of victory in the war on terrorism. The danger is that if the world's response to the growing new threat of annihilation is war, the result will be new acts of annihilation. Blair has won a seat in the war councils with his backing for the United States. Perhaps at some dire turning point in the future, he will use his influence to speak up for restraint. The world is sick. It cannot be cured with America's new war. The ways of peace—adopted not as a distant goal but as a practical necessity in the present—are the only cure.

Seven Million at Risk

NOVEMBER 5, 2001

THE HORRORS THAT have been sprung upon the world since September 11 have come with a rapidity that threatens to overwhelm the capacity of the imagination to respond, not to speak of the capacity of governments to frame policies that make sense.

No sooner had the Trade Center fallen and the Pentagon been attacked than the United States was declaring war; no sooner had the United States declared war than it was at war; no sooner was the United States at war than someone was attacking the United States with "weapons-grade" anthrax. The fifth week of the crisis has proceeded likewise. No sooner was anthrax arriving in mailboxes around the nation than still another horror—one that may yet prove the greatest of the entire story—was upon us: the prospect that millions of Afghans could starve to death this winter. On October 12 Mary Robinson, former President of Ireland and now the United Nations commissioner for human rights, sounded a sharp, clear warning. She called for a halt to the bombing of Afghanistan in order to permit humanitarian aid—above all, food—to be sent into Afghanistan before the winter snows cut off access to the population. "It is a very, very urgent situation," she noted. "It is very hard to get convoys of food in when there is a military campaign. . . . You have millions of people, they say up to 7 million, at risk." And she asked, "Are we going to preside over deaths from starvation of hundreds of thousands, maybe millions of people this winter because we did not use the window of opportunity?" Her words, though widely quoted around the world, went almost entirely unreported in the United States. The next day, among the thirty or so newspapers that the Lexis/Nexis database of newspapers calls major, only one—the *San Francisco Chronicle*—saw fit to mention it, and none of the major television networks did. (The day after that, Steven Erlanger briefly mentioned her comments in the *New York Times* in a story about eroding support in Germany for the bombing.) Not until four days later, when an American bomb destroyed a Red Cross warehouse in Kabul and humanitarian groups joined Robinson's call for a bombing halt, did the appeal begin to get attention in this country.

That a catastrophe was developing was not news—or should not have been. The combination of a decade of war by Afghan fighters against the Soviet Union, the civil war that followed the Soviet defeat, the extreme misrule of the victors in that war, the Taliban, and four years of drought have destroyed Afghanistan's ability to feed and care for itself. Humanitarian groups whose aid was already keeping substantial numbers of people alive have been warning of the gathering disaster as it has unfolded. After September 11, foreign aid personnel, advised by the Taliban that it could no longer assure their safety, withdrew from the country. Soon, the nations surrounding Afghanistan closed their borders to refugees. On September 19, Dominic Nutt, the emergency officer for the relief group Christian Aid, told the *Guardian*, "It's as if a mass grave has been dug behind millions of people. We can drag them back from it or push them in." On September 24, two weeks before the military campaign began, the UN warned in a report that "a humanitarian crisis of stunning proportions is unfolding in Afghanistan," and Secretary General Kofi Annan appealed for assistance to head off "the world's worst humanitarian disaster." On October 5 twenty relief organizations again reminded the world that Afghanistan was on the "brink of disaster." "It must be remembered," the statement said, "that these potential refugees are currently trapped inside a closed country." Two days later, the bombing began, and the vast internal migration from the cities to inaccessible rural parts of Afghanistan began. The new element introduced by Robinson's appeal was her delineation of the terrible significance of the bombing campaign in view of the deadline for assistance imposed by approaching winter.

The principal reason for saving the lives of the Afghans must, of course, be those lives themselves. Avenging thousands of innocents in America cannot take precedence over saving millions of innocents in Afghanistan. To say this is to make a moral point, but it is also more than a moral point. The humanitarian crisis of course arrives in the middle of a global military crisis and a political crisis. These last two—and the relationship between them—have dominated public attention and policy in the United States. What, we have been asking, is the outlook for military success in the "war on terrorism"? Will overthrowing the Taliban reduce or increase the terrorist threat? If they are overthrown, who will follow them? Will military success in Afghanistan spell political defeat in Pakistan and/or Saudi Arabia, where brittle, repressive regimes face strong opposition from Muslim extremists? These questions, echoing issues that arose in the Vietnam War, are important, but the answers to every one of them, we can now suddenly see, will depend on whether mass starvation can be headed off in Afghanistan. The spectacle of US special forces roving through a land of the dead and the dying in search of Osama bin Laden is as absurd a prescription for policy as it is offensive to decency.

A reversal of American policy is necessary. At present, political goals have been treated as a footnote to military goals (George W. Bush did not drop his opposition to nation-building in Afghanistan until a week after he ordered the bombing campaign), and humanitarian goals have been treated as a footnote to political goals. (The piteously inadequate food drops from US planes is the embodiment of this footnote.) This policy must be stood precisely on its head. Whatever the operational details, the humanitarian crisis must dominate. The bombing should stop, and a new policy—perhaps one of armed humanitarian intervention on the ground—should be adopted. Such a policy would replace the current iron fist in a humanitarian velvet glove with a helping human hand in a glove of chain mail. Not nation-building but nation-saving—the physical salvation of Afghan lives—must be the controlling consideration. Only if this humanitarian effort is successful can a political policy succeed—whether in Afghanistan itself, in Islamic opinion or in world opinion.

And only if these humanitarian and political goals are accomplished will the war on terrorism—whose importance, in our anthrax-menaced world, has become greater than ever—have any chance of going well.

Politics and War

NOVEMBER 19, 2001

HAWK AND DOVE agree: The war in Afghanistan is not going well. Hawks point to the resilience of the Taliban, which has "surprised" Rear Adm. John Stufflebeem by not collapsing yet. Doves point to the suffering of the civilian population, who face American bombing, Taliban repression and the prospect of mass starvation all at the same time. The problem goes deeper, however, than the unexpected toughness of the foe and stray bombs. It lies in an underlying contradiction in US policy. In a word, the Administration's military policy is at odds with its political policy. And in a war on terrorism—as distinct from a war on a state—it is politics, not military force, that will probably decide the outcome. For it is politics that will determine the size of the terrorist groups' most important asset, namely their pool of available recruits; it is politics that will decide how many countries will actively participate in the international police effort that must be the backbone of any global antiterrorism campaign; and it is politics that will decide how long support for the war will last in public opinion, including opinion on the home fronts.

To understand what is going wrong and why, we must look back at the origins of the war and its declared objectives. They were to uproot the networks of terrorists that sponsored the September 11 attacks, and, more particularly, to capture the alleged leader of those networks, Osama bin Laden. In the weeks leading up to the bombing, let us recall, a debate on strategy was conducted within the Administration and in the press. At issue was the scope of the war. Should it be extended beyond Afghanistan—perhaps to Iraq? The decision was to restrict it to Afghanistan, at least for the time being. Was it necessary to overthrow the Taliban regime—could the terrorist networks be attacked with the Taliban in place? This question was perhaps more extensively debated than any other. One problem was that terrorist groups were located in as many as fifty countries, not in Afghanistan alone. Another problem was that if you overthrew the Taliban, you would have to install another government—an undertaking that would constitute nation-building, which Bush had promised to avoid. Nor had the issue been publicly resolved when the bombing began. As noted in an earlier week on this page, Defense Secretary Donald Rumsfeld's articulation of American goals—to "create conditions for sustained antiterrorist action and humanitarian relief"—was surprisingly unambitious. There was no mention of overthrowing the Taliban, not to speak of any vow to create a substitute regime.

And yet as the bombing proceeded, it gradually became clear that overthrowing the Taliban was, after all, a goal of policy. Rumsfeld went as far as to remark that it might not be possible for the United States to capture bin Laden at all. On the other hand, he noted, overthrowing the Taliban was something that was within our power. The United States at that moment seemed to have abandoned what it wanted to do in favor of what it *could* do. A twofold strategy emerged. Its first goal was to support the Taliban's enemies, the Northern Alliance. Unfortunately, the Alliance members, most of whom belong to Uzbek and Tajik ethnic minorities, had misgoverned the country in the early 1990s. Accordingly, it was thought necessary to foster resistance to the Taliban among the dominant, Pashtun ethnic group in the south. The hope was that the Pashtun southerners—among whom the repressive Taliban were widely unpopular—would seize the opportunity of the US bombing to rebel. Then a coalition of anti-Taliban northerners and anti-Taliban southerners would ally to create a government friendly to the United States, whose military efforts could then cease.

This hope has been dashed by events. The bombing, far from prompting an anti-Taliban rebellion has, according to all reports, rallied popular support to the previously hated regime. Rarely has the destruction of political opportunity by military action been more clearly displayed. The extent of the reversal was revealed when Pakistan, under US direction, organized a meeting of anti-Taliban Afghan leaders. They promptly issued a call for a halt in the bombing—not, we must suppose, the reaction the United States was looking for. The change in political climate was further illustrated by the case of the Pashtun leader Abdul Haq, who entered the country from Pakistan to launch a rebellion but instead was captured and executed by the Taliban. There had in any case been something unreal about the expectation that the Taliban—more a social movement than a government— would collapse. "What is a government?" The Foreign Minister of Pakistan, Abdul Sattar, shrewdly inquired. "It has organs, it introduces a certain discipline in a country. But the government has simply ceased to exist in Afghanistan. . . . so it's not a matter of supplanting a state; it's a matter of rebuilding one from scratch." The Taliban was not, he said, "something that can be destroyed right away, because the government doesn't exist, in a way."

In response to these disappointments, many commentators have suggested, in effect, that a political strategy should be dispensed with altogether. Military victory alone will do. In the words of *Washington Post* columnist Charles Krauthammer, the goal of US policy now should be solely "destroying Al Qaeda and the Taliban" with military force. What comes after, he writes, is "an interesting problem. But it comes after." Senator John McCain called for heavier bombing and the introduction of ground troops.

These recommendations have the virtue of being practicable. The United States can unquestionably defeat the Taliban in a ground war and occupy Afghanistan. But politics will not disappear because it has been ignored. The state that is already missing in Afghanistan will still be missing. The Taliban and Al Qaeda will certainly remain as an underground force, exacting a steady price from the occupying armies. The English governed Northern Ireland for a quarter-century without being able to stop the terrorism there. And yet the cost of ending an occupation without creating a new government would be equally high, for there is no reason to suppose that Afghanistan, embittered by military defeat and foreign occupation, would not, once free of the occupier, return to its old ways of tolerating and supporting terrorism. Meanwhile, occupation of a Muslim country by US forces would be an outrage to Muslim opinion and a recruiting poster for terrorist organizations throughout the Middle East, which would almost certainly gain in strength. The United States can win the war in Afghanistan, but only at the cost of losing its war on terrorism.

Niceties

WHEN I BEGAN this column after September 11, I chose to name it "Letter From Ground Zero" because it seemed to me that at the heart of the new darkness that had descended upon the world was the peril of annihilation posed by weapons of mass destruction, including, above all, nuclear weapons. The weapon of mass destruction that has actually been used, of course, has been "weaponized" anthrax—delivered, however, only in minuscule amounts. The world awaits the terrorists' decision whether to follow up these retail murders with mass murder.

Meanwhile, the news media in this country, as if in obedience to some secret signal, are suddenly awash in stories dealing with nuclear weapons and nuclear danger. The discussion has developed with stunning rapidity, leading in some quarters to calls for the use of nuclear weapons of a kind not heard since the Cold War—if then. The stories come in two categories: warnings of attacks upon the United States and warnings of attacks by the United States. A raft of stories described the unpreparedness of the Nuclear Regulatory Commission for an attack on American nuclear reactors—attacks that could contaminate thousands of square miles. An article in *The New Yorker* by Seymour Hersh is the most detailed of many that discuss the danger that Pakistan's nuclear arsenal will fall into the hands of Islamic extremists, whether through theft by disaffected elements of the Pakistani nuclear establishment or by the overthrow of the military dictator President Pervez Musharraf. Musharraf, for his part, arrested Bashiruddin Mahmood, a leader for more than thirty years of Pakistan's nuclear weapons program and, more recently, a fervent and active supporter of the Taliban. A story in the *New York Times* offered an unnerving glimpse into the mentality of Islamic nuclear extremism. Mahmood, it reports, is the author of a book distressingly titled *The Mechanics of Doomsday and Life After Death* and also believes that the world's energy crisis can perhaps be solved by tapping the energy of genies—"beings made of fire" described in the Koran. A cover story by Gregg Easterbrook in *The New Republic* called "The Big One" offers an overview of the dangers of nuclear terrorism.

The most alarming stories, however, have been those warning of a direct nuclear attack by Osama bin Laden's organization. His passionate desire to acquire nuclear weapons has long been known, if little noticed. In the trial of those engaged in the 1998 bombing of the US embassies in Kenya and Tanzania, one of his operatives described his failed attempt to buy a cylinder of enriched uranium. In October, UPI's Richard Sale disclosed that according to "a half-dozen serving and former US Government and intelligence officials," the Bush Administration was concerned that "accused terrorist mastermind Osama bin Laden might try to use a small nuclear weapon in a super-spectacular strike to decapitate the US political leadership." The other day, George W. Bush made the concern official: Bin Laden, he said, is "seeking chemical, biological, and nuclear weapons." Bush notably gave no assurance that bin Laden did not already have nuclear weapons. "If he doesn't have them, we will work hard to make sure he doesn't," he said. "If he does, we'll make sure he doesn't deploy them."

Visions of American cities blown to kingdom come have reminded many of America's own very large arsenal of nuclear weapons. Might it be useful in the circumstances? Some commentators think it will be. We are not condemned merely to be the victims of mass destruction, they point out; we can be the perpetrators of it as well. I was alerted to one of these proposals by an unexpected source—the *New York Post*'s gossip columnist Liz Smith. She wished to commend an article in *Time* magazine by Charles Krauthammer, who, she noted with approval, wanted the United States to wage "total war" against its new enemies. "Have we told Iraq, the Saudis and Pakistan," she asked, that "if there is a nuclear attack . . . by anyone, we will hold them accountable because they have harbored and created these terrorists? We could wipe these countries off the map, and they should be very afraid of that." Krauthammer lived up to Smith's billing. The Bush administration's policy of trying to avoid civilian casualties might have to go by the board, he thought. In the "total war" he wanted, the distinction was a "nicety" that the United States could no longer afford. Krauthammer had only one country—Iraq—slated for annihilation. In the Gulf War, he claimed, the Administration of Bush Senior had warned President Saddam Hussein that if he used biological or chemical weapons he would be met with weapons that would "wipe Iraq off the face of the earth." Krauthammer wanted to know whether we were still ready to do this in the event of a terrorist use of a nuclear weapon on our soil. "If we are not prepared to wage total war we risk disaster on a scale we have never seen and can barely imagine," he wrote. Another commentator, *The New Republic*'s Easterbrook, had an entire region—the Islamic Middle East—in his sights. At the end of an appearance on *Greenfield at Large* on CNN, he announced that he wanted to leave his audience "with one message." It was that "the search for terrorist atomic weapons would be of great benefit to the Muslim peoples of the world in addition to . . . people of the United States and Western Europe, because if an atomic warhead goes off in Washington—say, in the current environment or anything like it—in the twenty-four hours that followed, a hundred million Muslims would die as US nuclear bombs rained down on every conceivable military target in a dozen Muslim countries."

"Wipe Iraq off the face of the earth," "a hundred million Muslims would die": Listening in shock to these phrases, it occurred to me that wiping a large nation "off the face of the earth"—not to speak of annihilating a dozen nations (and doing so merely because they had "harbored" terrorists)—is something that has never been done. To be fair, Krauthammer and Easterbrook wanted to consider the act only in the context of retaliation, and neither stated unequivocally that he would counsel actually carrying out the threat even then. On the other hand, neither pointed out that the deed they described would, if enacted, be a crime outside all human experience and would blacken the name of the United States in human memory forever. The darkness deepens. Have just two months of "war on terrorism" brought us to this?

In Hindsight

THE SUDDEN COLLAPSE of the Taliban in most of
Afghanistan is one of those events that seem to have been
designed by the fates to teach policy-makers and pundits
humility. The collapse came, of course, as a surprise; but it was
also something more: It arrived in the teeth of almost universal
opinion that it was not possible so soon. If there was one thing
that the predictors in and out of government—very much
including, I regret to say, this Letter—were agreed upon, it was
that the campaign to unseat the Taliban (the prelude to attacking
Al Qaeda) was going to last a long time—"years, not weeks or
months" in the words of Secretary of Defense Donald Rumsfeld, who noted that the formula could mean up to twenty-three
months. Hawks and doves in the newsmedia agreed. The hawks
said: The bombing isn't working; therefore the United States
must send in ground troops. Bombing alone, *The New Republic*
editorialized, could not achieve US objectives, even in combination with attacks on the ground by the Northern Alliance, of
which the magazine wrote, "Of all the proxies the United States

has enlisted over the past half-century, the Northern Alliance may be the least prepared to attain America's battlefield objectives." *The Weekly Standard* agreed. The real problem, the editors believed, was to enlist the Pashtun tribe in the south in the fight—something that would be possible only "if we are not dependent on the Northern Alliance for ground power." Therefore only "a significant deployment (in the tens of thousands) of American ground forces to the country" would serve.

Doves argued: The bombing isn't working, therefore stop the bombing and step up humanitarian aid instead, both for its own sake and because it will head off the increase in terrorism likely to accompany a war in a starving land. Here I can quote my own words against myself. The problem, I wrote in this Letter, was that American military strategy was at odds with its political strategy. In the first days of the war, I noted, the Administration had hoped for an anti-Taliban rebellion in its southern stronghold. The Taliban refused to permit Western journalists to enter Afghanistan, and information was sparse. Yet the capture of one anti-Taliban leader (Abdul Haq) injected from Pakistan and the ejection of another (Ahmed Karzai), among other events, suggested that this policy was failing. But above all, "the bombing, far from prompting an anti-Taliban rebellion, has, according to all reports, rallied popular support to the previously hated regime." History offered many supporting examples of peoples, including the Germans in World War II and the Vietnamese in the Vietnam War, whose will was stiffened rather than broken by bombing. On the basis of this assumption, a host of conclusions seemed to follow: If bombing was solidifying opposition to the United States, the war would last a long time; the humanitarian crisis would worsen; a large ground force probably would be sent in; the age-old Afghan hatred of foreign occupiers would be inflamed, and guerrilla war would ensue; anger at the United States would build around the Islamic world, and terrorism would increase; some Islamic regimes, especially that of nuclear-armed Pakistan, might even fall into extremist hands.

Even the Taliban, it appears, shared in the widespread misconception. Its spokesmen repeatedly threatened that the real war against America would begin only when it invaded on the ground.

The fates decided otherwise. If journalists were to devote their columns to correcting their previous misjudgments, the opinion pages of the papers would be filled with little else; yet nearly universal error does seem to call for at least some reflection by somebody. With the sharper (we can hope) vision of hindsight, it appears that the main mistake was to imagine, on the basis of a few scraps of information (the capture and execution of Haq, and so forth), that we could know what the temper of the people of Afghanistan was. Even after the fact firm judgments seem risky, yet on the basis of subsequent news reports it appears that many people hated the Taliban far more than they hated the bombing.

The collapse of the Taliban lines outside Kabul was perhaps not surprising. The Gulf War had made it clear that troops deployed in fixed positions in open terrain cannot long survive the effectively unlimited violence of American air power. Like the US troops entering Kuwait, the troops of the Northern Alliance faced little resistance when they finally breached Taliban lines. It was what happened next that amazed. The Alliance forces, whose warring factions had turned much of Kabul to rubble just six years before, were nevertheless greeted by many as saviors. Three symbols of liberation were immediately flashed around the world: men shaving unwanted beards; women casting off the tent-like burqas; children flying kites. Meanwhile, it turned out that the Taliban had simply quit the city. Only future investigation will reveal the reasons for their decision, but in the meantime it looks as though they knew that a fight in the streets of Kabul would be doomed with a hostile population at their backs.

A secondary factor seems to have played an important role—the traditional Afghan practice of deciding military confrontations through side-switching in brokered deals. In these deals, the losing side trades in its readiness to cease resistance for leniency or a share in power in the new dispensation. The practice, which permits some of the losers to join the victors, gives exceptional force to the urge to place oneself on the winning side. The Taliban came to power in Afghanistan largely through such deals, and they appear to have lost it in much of the country in the same way.

Of course, the war goes on. Overthrowing the Taliban (still in control of the cities of Kandahar and Kunduz as I write) is one thing; the founding of a new government, another. The same revolving door that ushered the Taliban in could usher in other distasteful characters soon. And American officials are already suggesting that in the "war on terrorism" there may be more wars to fight. But let us leave these questions for another time.

Is there anything to be learned? Use historical analogies sparingly. Reserve judgment when facts are unavailable. Respect the mystery of the will of peoples. Their decisions, can, when made, astonish the world.

A Chain Reaction

"IT IS ALMOST impossible even now to describe what actually happened in Europe on August 4, 1914," Hannah Arendt wrote in 1950, in words that also seem to apply, with uncanny aptness, to September 11, 2001. "The days before and the days after the first world war are separated not like the end of an old and the beginning of a new period but like the day before and the day after an explosion. . . . [That] explosion seems to have touched off a chain reaction in which we have been caught ever since and which nobody seems to be able to stop." The chain reaction was the abrupt, unstoppable plunge into the protracted, unprecedented savagery of the two world wars and the two great totalitarian regimes, Soviet and Nazi, of the century's first half. It's still too soon to know whether September 11 (let us avoid the trivializing, disrespectful notation "nine eleven") will touch off a comparable—or worse—spiral of violence in the twenty-first century. An "explosion" we have definitely had; whether an unstoppable "chain reaction" of violence has been triggered we do not know. Yet already the elements of not one but at least three distinct possible kinds of disaster have appeared with astonishing swiftness.

First (to list them briefly), is the threat of a much wider conventional war. Even as the war in Afghanistan still rages, voices in and out of government are calling for new wars against new countries. The targets and justifications for attacking them shift with dizzying rapidity. The war most often mentioned is one to overthrow the regime of President Saddam Hussein of Iraq. The justification first given was a possible connection to the September 11 attack or the anthrax attack that followed; but when this justification seemed to fade (hard facts are impossible to come by), a new one—Saddam's refusal to let UN inspectors into his country to search for weapons of mass destruction—was brought forward. Next, we were hearing from inside sources that the targets might in fact be Somalia or Sudan. (The attack on Iraq would be considered later.) Meanwhile, other crises are sucked into the vortex. In the latest round of violence between Israel and Palestine, Israel, seeking to associate its own war on terror with the American one, has responded to the suicide bombings by the Islamic organization Hamas by attacking the head of the Palestinian Authority, Yasir Arafat. If this development leads to the collapse or expulsion of Arafat from Palestine and definitively ends hopes for a Palestinian state, it could rouse the fury of the Islamic world against the United States and Israel alike, and bring on the full-scale "clash of civilizations" predicted by the political scientist Samuel Huntington.

Second, the Bush Administration has responded to the terrorist threat with executive measures that some are calling the most serious threat to civil liberties in recent memory. The list already includes a roundup of more than a thousand people without charges; eavesdropping on conversations between terrorism-related suspects and their attorneys; a huge, ill-defined expansion of wiretapping in the United States; and, of course, the creation by presidential order of military tribunals that try and execute noncitizens in secret by majority vote. If, as George W. Bush says, we must not allow terrorists to use our freedom to attack us, then how much less should we destroy our own freedom in order to attack the terrorists? Freedom is not some glittering abstraction that hovers in the air; it is the Constitution and the rights it guarantees to citizens. To lose these will be to lose the war no matter how many terrorists the United States kills in Afghanistan.

Third, looming over all these developments is a threat unknown in 1914—the use of weapons of mass destruction against the United States, by the United States, or both. Osama bin Laden has stated that he possesses nuclear weapons ("as a deterrent"), and Administration sources are telling reporters that there is reason to fear that he may have radiological weapons (which use conventional explosives to spread radioactive materials across a wide area). Meanwhile, Defense Secretary Donald Rumsfeld has pointedly declined to rule out first-use of nuclear weapons by the United States at some point in the conflict.

What protection does the world have now against a new chain reaction, in which these dangers will feed on and produce one another? To the people—a large majority, according to the polls—who favor present policy, the protection probably seems adequate, or as good as it can be, but to someone like me, who, as this Letter has made clear, opposes both the war abroad and the inroads on liberty at home, Arendt's description of a world in which events are outrunning understanding and response seems frighteningly current. Neither widening war abroad nor loss of liberty at home nor the danger of mass destruction seems to have stirred a response anywhere near the level of the danger. We seem to be gliding in a kind of glassy calm toward a multitude of horrors. There is incontrovertible evidence—including a shocking series of photographs in the *New York Times*—that our new ally the Northern Alliance has been executing prisoners of war, but there is little reaction in the United States. Serious allegations have also been made that the Alliance, with the help of American bombers, has massacred hundreds of prisoners in the city of Mazar-i-Sharif. The Administration has shown no interest in discovering the truth. The nation's shock was intense when Americans were killed in the September 11 attacks. But reports that villages have been destroyed by US bombing in Afghanistan go uninvestigated. Asked about the press coverage of the subject, Brit Hume of Fox News commented, "The fact that some people are dying, is that really news? And is it news to be treated in a semi-straight-faced way? I think not." The Administration is clear cutting constitutional protections, but few legislators take an interest.

It's one thing to face possible disasters; another to let them draw near without protest or action, as if in a trance or dream. "Nothing which was being done . . . no matter how many people knew and foretold the circumstances, could be undone or prevented," Arendt wrote of the earlier period. The question now arises whether an opposition today can find the ground on which to take its stand. Or will "every event," as Arendt wrote of the earlier time, "have the finality of a last judgment, a judgment that was passed neither by God nor by a devil, but looked rather like the expression of some unredeemably stupid fatality"?

The Wars on Terrorism

JANUARY 7, 2002

AT THE OUTSET of the war on terrorism, President Bush announced a doctrine: Regimes that harbor terrorists will be dealt with as severely as the terrorists themselves. Three months later, the Taliban regime that then ruled Afghanistan is gone, and Washington is scanning the horizon for other regimes to attack. The government of Iraq is the one most frequently mentioned.

There was no sign back in September that Bush imagined that other countries might claim comparable rights, but that is what has happened. On December 13 terrorists attacked the Indian Parliament, killing seven. India announced its belief that extremist Islamic groups in Pakistan were responsible and that they had the backing of the Pakistani government, America's new ally in Afghanistan. A spokesman for Pakistan further enraged Indian opinion by answering that India may have staged the attack upon itself. India's home minister, L.K. Advani, then accused Pakistan of having "the temerity to try to wipe out the entire political leadership of India." In holding the Pakistani government responsible for terrorism by groups in Pakistan, India consciously adopted the US doctrine to the letter. Now it is contemplating military action.

Just how deep India's debt is to the American example is revealed by, among other things, an article by Brahma Chellaney, professor of security studies at India's Center for Policy Research. He wants the December 13 attack to "shape India's response to terrorism in the same unmistakable way that September 11 has defined America's." The solution he has in mind is the use of force and other unilateral measures. Just as the United States pulled out of the ABM treaty, Chellaney writes, so India should pull out of its Indus River Water Treaty with Pakistan. "The resultant water crisis," he hopefully suggests, "will help foment internal disturbances and contribute to Pakistan's self-destruction." But shouldn't Pakistan's nuclear arsenal induce caution, he wonders? In phrases borrowed directly from the high texts of US nuclear theology, he answers that there is nothing to worry about, because India can answer "any level" of attack with a "higher level." So if, for example, Pakistan destroys ten of India's greatest cities with nuclear weapons, India presumably can destroy twenty of Pakistan's, and everything will be fine.

Alarmed, perhaps, by such patent lunacy—and also by the danger that America's own coalition against terror, in which India and Pakistan have vied for leading roles, will be busted up—the White House, through its spokesman Ari Fleischer, counsels "restraint." India is unimpressed. Counsel of restraint from a nation that has just overthrown the government of one country and now has five or six more in its gunsights can hardly be expected to carry weight with one whose Parliament has been attacked, as it believes, by its enemy of almost half a century.

A similar pattern of events has unfolded in the Middle East, where terrorist attacks on Israel have been conducted with increasing frequency. There, it is of course Israel that places itself in the role of the United States; the leader of the Palestinian Authority Yasir Arafat that Israel places in the role of the Taliban; and the terrorist organization Hamas that Israel places in the role of the Al Qaeda network in Afghanistan. Prime Minister of Israel Ariel Sharon, employing the Bush formula for purposes that are longstanding, declared Arafat and his regime "directly responsible" for the terrorism and proceeded to cut off all contact with him and then to wage war on the structures of his Authority. If India's war threatens to destroy the US alliance with Pakistan, Israel's threatens to collapse the US coalition in the entire Middle East, whose peoples care much more about the suffering of Palestine under Israeli occupation than they do about anything that Al Qaeda might do to the United States. Weapons of mass destruction are involved in this part of the world, too. Israel has an arsenal of some 200 nuclear weapons, and Iran and Iraq reportedly are seeking to build nuclear arsenals. It has also been reported that two of the scientists who helped build Pakistan's bomb have had wide-ranging discussions on weapons of mass destruction with Al Qaeda in Afghanistan. How long will it be before one of these entities— whether a state or something else—obtains the weapons it seeks, and what will happen in the Middle East then?

The American model has had a clear influence in several other parts of the world. The savage Russian war in Chechnya long predates September 11. Russia had its September 11 on September 9–16, 1999, when three apartment buildings were destroyed and more than 200 people were killed in explosions whose perpetrators have never been identified but that Vladimir Putin attributed to Chechen terrorists. "After the first shock passed, it turned out that we were living in an entirely different country, in which almost no one dared talk about a peaceful, political resolution of the crisis with Chechnya," human rights activist Sergei Kovalev wrote last year. Describing the national mood that then carried Putin into the presidency, he wrote, "War and only war is the solution!" The war that followed was criticized by the United States and its Western allies—until September 11, when the White House announced that that conflict was also a war on terrorism.

China, too, has joined in the trend. It has broken its customary silence regarding its repression of the Islamic Uighur movement in its western province of Xinjiang, announcing that since our invasion of Afghanistan, it has arrested 2,500 "separatists." Even tiny Nepal has gotten into the act. It has ended talks with the Maoist insurgency there and turned to military measures.

When the Bush Administration began its war on terrorism, announcing that if you weren't with us you were against us, did it imagine that from the dizzying heights of its sole superpowerdom it would command the nations, rewarding some, raining bombs on others, and dominating all, according to its sole interest and pleasure? The nations have had other ideas. Preferring American practice to American preaching, they have taken up arms in their own causes, just as previously many built nuclear arsenals whose use again urgently threatens the world. We have not one unified war on terrorism but many clashing wars. It's hard to say which are more dangerous—those that, like Israel's, seek to join the American one or those that, like India's, seem to undercut it. All are burning out of control. For now, the instruments that alone might stop them—negotiation, treaties, a readiness to compromise, measures of disarmament—have been cast aside.

Disarmament Wars

FEBRUARY 25, 2002

LONG BEFORE THE atomic bomb turned night into day in the desert of Alamogordo in July 1945, it was an idea in the minds of scientists, who deeply pondered the political and moral dilemma they were about to impose on the world. With few exceptions, they arrived at a basic conclusion. The great physicist Niels Bohr articulated it well when he said, "We are in a completely new situation that cannot be resolved by war." The reasons were clear and inescapable. In the first place, thanks to the unlimited destructive power of nuclear weapons, nuclear war "cannot be won and must never be fought," as Ronald Reagan was to put it much later. In the second place, the knowledge on which the bomb was based was destined, like all knowledge, to spread. In the long run, there would be no "secret" of the bomb. The conclusion was equally clear: If nuclear danger was to be contained or lifted, the task had to be accomplished by political means—above all, by international agreements.

The first and most ambitious of these—the Baruch plan, which was put forward by President Truman and called for the abolition of nuclear weapons—was rejected by the Soviet Union, which then put forward a plan that was rejected by the United States. The arms race that the scientists had hoped to head off began. Nevertheless, for the rest of the century the world followed the scientists' advice: Except on one occasion, no nuclear power used force to stop another power from getting nuclear weapons. The pattern was set in the late 1940s, when the United States declined to launch a preemptive attack on the Soviet Union in the years before it got the bomb. In the early days of the Soviet nuclear buildup, President Eisenhower likewise rejected what he called "preventive war." "How could you have one," he said at a press conference, "if one of its features would be several cities lying in ruins, several cities where many, many thousands of people would be dead and injured and mangled?" The pattern held when China launched its nuclear weapons program: Neither the United States nor the Soviet Union launched a preemptive attack. The one exception was the Israeli attack in June 1981 on a reactor that Iraq was using in its nuclear-weapons program.

All other attempts to stop the spread of nuclear weapons or reduce existing arsenals have been diplomatic and political. They include the Nuclear Nonproliferation Treaty, which came into force in 1974, the SALT and START treaties, under which the nuclear arsenals of the United States and the Soviet Union, and then Russia, have been cut by half, the Comprehensive Test Ban Treaty, and the Anti-Ballistic Missile Treaty of 1972.

In his State of the Union address on January 29, George W. Bush, in one of the sharpest and most significant policy shifts of the nuclear age, overthrew this consensus of more than a half-century. He announced his decision to do just the thing that

Niels Bohr said was impossible: to try to solve the nuclear dilemma by waging war. His words left no room for doubt about his intentions. After lumping together Iraq, Iran, and North Korea with the odd locution "axis of evil," he said, "I will not wait on events while dangers gather. I will not stand by as peril draws closer and closer. The United States of America will not permit the world's most dangerous regimes to threaten us with the world's most destructive weapons."

The historic importance of the shift was concealed by the context in which Bush placed it, namely the "war on terrorism." A radically new policy was presented as a mere expansion of an existing one. The segue came when he said that the evil-axis nations "could provide these arms to terrorists, giving them the means to match their hatred." After the fall of the Taliban, much ink was spilled speculating on what "phase two" of the war on terrorism might be. Would the United States chase Al Qaeda into Indonesia, Pakistan, Somalia, Lebanon? Now it turns out that phase two is not a war on terrorism at all but a whole series of much larger wars to stop the spread of weapons of mass destruction—history's first disarmament wars.

The new nonproliferation strategy is in truth only the culminating move in a much broader shift in American policy from diplomacy to force—or to put it more plainly, from peace to war. An accompanying move has been the widely uncommented-upon US exit from the entire structure of nuclear arms control treaties that were built over the past thirty years or so. In 1999 the Senate refused to ratify the test ban treaty. Late last year, the Bush Administration gave notice that its continuing reduction of strategic nuclear arms would occur outside any treaty, putting an end to START. A few weeks later, the Administration announced its withdrawal from the Anti-Ballistic Missile treaty, the better to build national missile defense. Only the Nuclear Nonproliferation Treaty, to which the United States belongs as a nuclear power, remains intact, and it has never managed to put any constraints on US behavior. Its raison d'être in the eyes of the United States has always been to constrain not the United States but the 182 nations that have agreed to forgo nuclear weapons. In any case, the new Bush policy clearly announces that the true prevention of proliferation is not to be any treaty but American attack.

These policies form a unity: The United States, safe behind its missile shield, will, at its sole discretion and unconstrained by treaties or even consultation with allies (there was no real consultation with the NATO countries on the new policy and no mention of NATO in Bush's address), protect its territory and impose its will in the world by using its unmatched military power to coerce or destroy, if possible by preemptive attack, every challenger.

Nothing Bush proposes, however, has undone the elementary truths that led Niels Bohr to warn, years ago, against trying to solve the nuclear dilemma by war. The ABM treaty can be torn up, but the laws of physics cannot. Smart bombs can destroy armies, but not even the most brilliant of them can remove a thought from a person's mind, or stop its conveyance to the mind of another. These are lessons that the world learned, however imperfectly, at the dawn of the nuclear age and that have been confirmed by more than a half-century of experience since. How many wars will be fought and how many lives will be lost before we learn them again?

Manhattan

APRIL 1, 2002

NEW YORK, THE city in which I was born and grew up and have lived all my life, and in which my children were born and have now grown up, was also the birthplace of the atomic bomb. The first practical steps toward building the bomb were taken at Columbia University, where the Hungarian physicist Leo Szilard and the Italian physicist Enrico Fermi, among others, did preliminary experiments demonstrating that a chain reaction of nuclear fission could be initiated.

Even in the first days of the nuclear age, Szilard, who, after helping create the bomb spent the rest of his life agitating to get rid of it, understood right away that the makers of the bomb could one day be its victims. In 1945 he wrote, "The position of the United States in the world may be adversely affected by their existence. . . . Clearly if such bombs are available, it will not be necessary to bomb our cities from the air in order to destroy them. All that is necessary is to place a comparatively small number in major cities and detonate them at some later time. . . . The long coastline, the structure of our society, and the heterogeneity of our population may make effective controls of such 'traffic' virtually impossible."

The next stop on the road to the bomb was Chicago, where, under the Chicago University sports stadium, the first chain reaction was loosed; and then it was on to Los Alamos, where the bomb was built, and to the Valley of the Journey of Death, where, on July 16, 1945, the first nuclear weapon was detonated. Still, the New York origins of the bomb were preserved for history in the name given to the enterprise: the Manhattan Project.

Now it's fifty-seven long years later. A lot has happened—among other things, acquisition of the bomb by seven other nations, the Cuban missile crisis, the Soviet collapse, and September 11. But humanity is still toiling through the Valley of the Journey of Death, currently with a burden on its collective back of 32,000 nuclear weapons. Not until this year, however, has Szilard's prophecy returned to disturb the sleep of New Yorkers. *Time* magazine recently disclosed that in October federal officials received a plausible report that a nuclear attack on New York by terrorists was in the works—perhaps with a ten-kiloton weapon they were told was missing from the Russian arsenal. "It was brutal," an official said of the experience. Meanwhile, we learned that the Bush Administration had set up a "shadow government" of officials hidden away in underground bunkers to keep the government operating in case of a nuclear attack on Washington.

The alarm proved—thank God!—to be false. But everyone knows that the next time it could be real. The news has prompted new mental exercises. A full-scale nuclear holocaust does not invite much detailed thought. Everything will be gone. What is there to think about? The reported peril from one bomb to New

York is a different matter. Thought and imagination, tutored by September 11, got more specific—more visceral, more tactical. At Hiroshima, I knew, survivors on the outer edges of the sphere of annihilation directed their steps into the countryside. There would be no such luck for the injured of sea-girt Manhattan, escapable only by a few bridges and tunnels. The psychiatrist Robert J. Lifton has quoted the description by a Hiroshima grocer of the people fleeing the city: "At a glance you couldn't tell whether you were looking at them from in front or in back . . . they held their arms [in front of them] . . . and their skin—not only on their hands but on their faces and bodies too—hung down." Not many people in that condition will get through, say, the Brooklyn Battery tunnel. When the Trade Center was hit on September 11, some people had the presence of mind to steal kayaks from sports stores and paddle to New Jersey. But these were vain thoughts, futile plans. Even this level of nuclear destruction—"low" in comparison to a general holocaust—seems to involve the imagination in defeat. Does someone want to crumple up this great and beautiful city and throw it into history's trashcan like a piece of Kleenex? Does someone want to put an end to the rough-edged but sweet New York life we have here? It appears that they may and that soon they may possess the means.

With these fears pervading the atmosphere, other news of the bomb was arriving—news not of nuclear attacks the United States might suffer but of nuclear attacks the United States might deliver upon others. Reports of the Administration's new Nuclear Posture Review reveal that it is not going to reduce the strategic arsenal down to about 2,000, as recently announced by George W. Bush; it is going to warehouse the "cut" weapons. It has also drawn up plans to expand nuclear weapons production, to design and build new varieties of nuclear warheads and, most shocking, to use nuclear weapons against at least seven countries: Russia, China, North Korea, Libya, Syria, Iraq, and Iran. Other countries are looking on with alarm—fearful that a monster, driven mad by righteous fury and dizzy with its own power, is rising out of the ashes of September 11 to bellow destruction to the world.

In short, at exactly the moment New York and Washington, reeling from the attacks of September 11, were awakening to their helplessness in the face of possible nuclear attack, our government was moving to relegitimize the use of nuclear weapons in general and throwing down the nuclear gauntlet to the Middle East in particular—the very part of the world from which New York and Washington and other cities most fear attack.

Did the decision-makers in Washington reflect, when they gave themselves the right to launch nuclear attacks on the Middle East and elsewhere, that they might inspire those targeted to do likewise to us? Did they forget that there is no defense against nuclear arms and no rescue for those attacked by them? Leo Szilard was right fifty-seven years ago. In the long run, nuclear destructive power is available to all, just as it menaces all. No country is omnipotent. None are invulnerable. What the United States has done to others at Hiroshima and Nagasaki—and what we may yet do to others at Teheran and Tripoli—others can do to us.

The offspring of the Manhattan Project are circling back toward Manhattan. Two towers of blue light rise where the towers of glass and steel once rose. What monument would be conceivable as the gravestone of all New York? What can we do to save our beloved, injured, perishable city?

The Growing Nuclear Peril

ON JUNE 12, 1982, one million people assembled in Central Park in New York City to call for a freeze of the nuclear arms race. In the years that followed, the Cold War waned and then ended, and the strategic nuclear arsenals of the United States and the Soviet Union were not only frozen but cut to about half of their peak. In the early post-Cold War years, it seemed conceivable that nuclear arms might be on their way to obsolescence, and nuclear danger pretty much dropped out of the public mind.

It's now clear that these hopes were ill founded. The nuclear dilemma was not going away; it was changing shape. Four years ago, I asked in a special issue of this magazine whether the nuclear arsenals of the Cold War were "merely a monstrous left-over from a frightful era that has ended, and will soon follow it into history, or whether, on the contrary, they are the seeds of a new, more virulent nuclear era." The seeds have now sprouted, and that new era is upon us in South Asia and elsewhere.

Today, twenty years after the June 12 demonstration, some of us who were present at the event believe that the time has come again for the public to make its voice heard in protest against the direction of nuclear policies, and we are therefore issuing the Urgent Call.* As one of its signatories, I wish to explain why I think this is necessary. Passages from the Call are in small capital print; the commentary is in ordinary type.

"DESPITE THE END OF THE COLD WAR, THE UNITED STATES PLANS TO KEEP LARGE NUMBERS OF NUCLEAR WEAPONS INDEFINITELY."

According to President George W. Bush, the recently signed Moscow Treaty, under which the United States and Russia have agreed to a limit on deployed strategic weapons of no more than 2,200 each, "liquidates the legacy of the Cold War." Rarely has more contradiction, misdirection, and confusion been compacted into a single phrase. Let us count the ways.

(1) The Cold War—the global ideological struggle between the United States and the Soviet Union—in fact ended definitively in 1991 with the disappearance of the Soviet Union from the face of the earth. The President at the time, Bush's father, told us so. As one Russian wag recently commented, "I'm tired of attending funerals for the Cold War." The Cold War is over. Long live the Cold War.

(2) Does liquidating the legacy of the Cold War then perhaps mean liquidating the nuclear arsenals that were built up in the name of that struggle? No. Not a single nuclear warhead will be dismantled under the treaty. Even the deployed

* See Appendix

weapons will, when the reductions are complete, be quite sufficient for either country to blow up the other many times over. It is better that the excess warheads will be in storage than on hairtrigger alert, but the move only reduces the overkill. All the kill remains. In other words, at the treaty's expiration, in 2012, more than two decades after the disappearance of the Soviet Union, the nuclear policies—as distinct from the active and alert force levels—of the two nations will not have changed in the slightest particular.

(3) If neither the Cold War nor its nuclear arsenals are being liquidated, does the treaty at least consolidate a postwar friendship between Russia and the United States? On the contrary, the United States has introduced a fresh note of suspicion into the relationship by insisting on storing rather than dismantling the "reduced" weapons in order to "hedge" against some undefined deterioration in relations with Russia—notwithstanding the new consultative relationship of Russia with NATO. One day, the United States thus declares to Russia, 2,200 nuclear weapons may not be enough for dealing with you; we may again need 10,000. That message is reinforced by a shortening of the usual six-month withdrawal time in treaties to three months.

(4) Does the treaty liquidate anything, then? Yes—nuclear arms control. The Bush Administration, which resisted putting even the Moscow agreement in treaty form, has let it be known that it intends no further arms control treaties with Russia. On June 13, the United States will formally withdraw from the Anti-Ballistic Missile treaty. The world, President

Bush is saying, has had all the nuclear disarmament it is going to get out of the end of the Cold War. But if the twice-announced end of that conflict cannot get Russia and the United States out of the trap of "mutual assured destruction," what can? Nothing is on the horizon. Woodrow Wilson fought the "war to end all wars." George Bush has signed an arms control treaty to end all arms control treaties.

"THE DANGERS POSED BY HUGE ARSENALS, THREATS OF USE, PRO-LIFERATION, AND TERRORISM ARE LINKED. . . ."

It's all a matter, as we've learned to say of the pre-September 11 intelligence failures, of connecting the dots. The failure of the end of the Cold War's political hostilities to bring with it the end of the Cold War's nuclear arsenals is a fact of prime importance for the era that is beginning. No longer justified as a remnant of the old era, they have now become the foundation stone of the new one. They relegitimize nuclear arsenals at lower levels. The plain message for the future is that in the twenty-first century, countries that want to be safe need large nuclear arsenals, even in the absence of present enemies. This of course is a formula for nuclear proliferation.

The place in the world to look today for a portrait of prolif-eration is South Asia, where India and Pakistan are closer to nuclear war than any two countries have been since the Cuban missile crisis, or perhaps ever. According to a recent government study, twelve million lives are at immediate risk. A multiple of that could be the eventual total. The world has scarcely begun to absorb the meaning of these figures. It is a crisis in which almost every conceivable form of violence and threat of violence is tied into a single knot. Up to a million men facing each other across an 1,800-mile border are primed for a World War I-style conventional war. Between them is a disputed territory, Kashmir. On that territory a liberation movement pits an indigenous Muslim minority against Indian repression in the part of Kashmir under its control. Extremist groups in Kashmir and supporters who cross the border from Pakistan to aid them add the incendiary ingredient of terrorism. In a deadly new combination, terrorism threatens to unbalance the balance of terror. The leaders of both countries—the dictator Pervez Musharraf of Pakistan and the head of the Hindu fundamentalist Bharatiya Janata Party, Prime Minister Atal Behari Vajpayee of India— have taken "tough" stands from which they can withdraw only at high political cost. In a groggy atmosphere of global inattention and inaction, the two nations drift toward nuclear war. Its outbreak would change history forever.

Even as the great powers' fresh embrace of their nuclear arsenals incites proliferation, proliferation (to further connect the dots) fuels the terrorist danger. A world of multiplying nuclear powers will be a world awash in nuclear materials. To give just one instance, it is known that the Pakistani nuclear-weapon scientist and Muslim fanatic Sultan Bashiruddin Mahmood has visited Osama bin Laden to talk over nuclear matters. A few months ago, bin Laden announced—falsely, we can only hope— that he possessed nuclear arms, and it is known that the Al Qaeda network has sought them. In a May article in *The New York Times Magazine*, complete with washed-out, vaguely postapocalyptic photographs of New York, Bill Keller reported that forestalling such an attack is now one of the highest priorities of the federal government.

The relegitimation of nuclear weapons in the toothless Moscow Treaty, the rising danger of nuclear war in South Asia and the spreading fear of nuclear terrorism in the United States and elsewhere are only the most recent harvest of danger—three new dots on the single, terrifying emerging map of the second nuclear age.

"SAFETY FROM NUCLEAR DESTRUCTION MUST BE OUR GOAL. WE CAN REACH IT ONLY BY REDUCING AND THEN ELIMINATING NUCLEAR ARMS UNDER BINDING AGREEMENTS."

The Bush Administration, which is acutely aware of the dangers of both nuclear terrorism and nuclear proliferation (Secretary of Defense Donald Rumsfeld has called the use of a weapon of mass destruction on American soil "inevitable"), has consistently turned to military force as its chosen remedy. Its formula for dealing with terrorism is to overthrow states that harbor terrorists. Its program for stopping proliferation is likewise overthrowing some states—perhaps beginning with the government of Iraq—that seek to engage in it. The new strategy has been codified in a new Nuclear Posture Review, which proposes a policy of "offensive deterrence," under which the United States threatens preemptive attack, including possible nuclear attack, against nations that acquire or threaten to use weapons of mass destruction. Disarmament has become an occasion for war. But force is more likely to incite proliferation than to end it. In a world whose great powers were committed to nuclear disarmament, the decision by other nations to forgo these weapons would be consistent with national self-respect. But in a world in which one self-designated enforcer of a two-tier nuclear system sits atop a mountain of nuclear bombs and threatens destruction of any regime that itself seeks to acquire them, such forbearance becomes national humiliation—a continuation of the hated colonial system of the past, or "nuclear apartheid," as the Indian government put it.

The Urgent Call, by contrast, proposes a return to the tested and proven path of negotiation, through which 182 countries have already agreed, under the terms of the Nuclear Nonproliferation Treaty, to stay out of the nuclear weapons business. The call raises the banner of a single standard: a world without nuclear weapons.

"WE THEREFORE CALL ON THE UNITED STATES AND RUSSIA . . . TO MOVE TOGETHER WITH THE OTHER NUCLEAR POWERS, STEP BY CAREFULLY INSPECTED AND VERIFIED STEP, TO THE ABOLITION OF NUCLEAR WEAPONS."

The goal of nuclear abolition, it is true, is ambitious, and the difficulties are mountainous. Many will say, as they have throughout the nuclear age, that it is unrealistic. They would perhaps be right if we lived in a static world. But events—in South Asia, in Central Asia, in the Middle East, in New York—are moving at breakneck pace, and the avenues to disaster are multiplying. A nuclear revival is under way. A revival of nuclear protest is needed to stop it.

The Path to Point B

SEPTEMBER 23, 2002

A YEAR THAT began (if we count by the new calendar whose Day One is September 11, 2001) with an attack on the United States by a terrorist group consisting mostly of Saudi Arabians headquartered in Afghanistan has ended with preparations for an attack by the United States on Iraq, a country that had no demonstrated involvement in September 11. The path from point A a year ago to point B now has been lengthy and circuitous. Along the way, a radically new conception of America's role in the world has been advanced by the Bush Administration. It has claimed nothing less than a right and a duty of the United States to assert military dominance—a Pax Americana—over the entire earth. Discussion along the way has been muted, but now a debate has begun. Its subject, however, has been not so much whether the United States should wage war on Iraq as whether it should wage the debate on the war, or—what is only a little bolder—whether the United States should first meet certain conditions (find allies, explain itself to Congress, win the support of the American public, make plans for Iraq's political

79

future) and only *then* wage the war. The debate proceeds backward from the conclusion to the arguments for it. The witnesses before the recent hearings of the Senate Foreign Relations Committee, for example, all favored "regime change" in Iraq; they disagreed only on how to go about it. This deliberately vague and slippery propaganda phrase blurs critical policy distinctions, creating an impression of consensus where none may really exist. At the hearings, the most hawkish witness was retired Lieut. Gen. Thomas McInerney, who advocated "blitz warfare" using "the Global Strike Task Force and Naval Strike Forces composed of over 1,000 land and sea-based aircraft plus a wide array of air and sea-launched cruise missiles" to launch "the most massive precision air campaign in history, achieving rapid dominance in the first seventy-two hours of combat, focused on regime-change targets." The most dovish was perhaps Morton Halperin, of the Council on Foreign Relations, who for now wanted no more than stricter enforcement of the regime of sanctions against Iraq.

A few voices—mostly Republican—have gone as far as to ask whether the war itself is a good idea. Even this question, however, cannot be adequately addressed without consideration of the Administration's larger assertion of the right to overthrow regimes by military force at its sole discretion. The case for or against the war against Iraq stands or falls on the wisdom of this claim.

The Administration did not present its policy directly or all at once. It advanced it gradually and stealthily, as if each expansion of US ambitions were merely an appendage to or necessary consequence of what is in fact only one of the policy's secondary aspects—the "war on terrorism." The first step in the process was the wording of that phrase. Almost all previous campaigns against terrorists had been defined not as wars but as police campaigns. By calling this campaign a "war," the Administration summoned the immense American military machine into action. And by identifying the target generically as "terrorism" rather than naming a specific foe, such as the Al Qaeda network, the Administration licensed military operations, covert as well as overt, anywhere in the world.

The second step was the decision to overthrow a government—the Taliban regime in Afghanistan. Difficult as it is to remember now, there was a debate within the Administration itself as to whether elimination of the Taliban was advisable. Soon after September 11, President Bush stated in his speech to Congress that he would "make no distinction between the terrorists who committed these acts and those who harbor them." The immediate question was whether he meant that the United States would assault not only the Al Qaeda network that had mounted the attack but also the Afghan regime. The curious fact is that the Administration never did announce that overthrow of the regime was its policy. If anything, it seemed to disavow the aim. When, just two days after the attack began, Deputy Defense Secretary Paul Wolfowitz stated that the aim of US policy should be "ending states who sponsor terrorism," Secretary of State Colin Powell went out of his way to disagree, stating that "ending terrorism is where I would like to leave it, and let Mr. Wolfowitz speak for himself." Shortly, the President appeared to back up Powell. After seeming briefly to hint agreement with Wolfowitz by commenting that he would "ask for the cooperation of citizens within Afghanistan who may be tired of having the Taliban in place," Bush sent out his press secretary, Ari Fleischer, to state unequivocally that American policy "is not designed to replace one regime with another regime." The debate was settled not by an announcement or explanation to the public but simply by the deed itself. The anaesthetic phrase "regime change" had not been launched, but the fact of it had become a reality. The United States was now officially in the business of overthrowing governments by military force.

The next step was to expand the definition of the war on terrorism to include stopping the proliferation of weapons of mass destruction. The occasion was Bush's State of the Union speech, in which he named Iran, Iraq, and North Korea, all of which are known to have or to have had programs to build weapons of mass destruction, as an "axis of evil." "The United States of America," he announced, "will not permit the world's most dangerous regimes to threaten us with the world's most destructive weapons." Nuclear proliferation has been a feature of the nuclear age since its beginning. Attempts to stop it—the policy of nonproliferation—have been an explicit goal of every Administration. However, the United States had always restricted itself to diplomatic and political means. For example, in the 1940s there was no preemptive strike against the nuclear-weapons program of Stalin, a dictator who had overseen the murder of tens of millions of his own citizens. The greatest success of the political approach has been the Nuclear Nonproliferation Treaty, under which 182 nations have agreed not to build nuclear arsenals. Now, however, nonproliferation has become a military undertaking. In a radical escalation, the war on terror had become—or been used to disguise—a war on weapons of mass destruction. No acknowledgment was made that the decision reversed several decades of policy. No argument was made that military means were superior to the diplomatic and political means that had always been employed in the past.

The main elements of the new policy were now in place: The United States asserted the right to use its unchallengeable military might, including its Global Strike Task Force, to overthrow governments by force if, in its view, they either harbored terrorists or attempted to acquire weapons of mass destruction. Vice President Cheney estimates the former category at some sixty nations. No definitive enumeration of the latter has been given, but the potential is great, inasmuch as there are many dozens of countries capable of building weapons of mass destruction should they choose to do so.

It remained to make a fuller declaration of the new policy. The statement came in the President's speech to the graduating class at West Point in June. The days of American reliance on "deterrence" and "containment," he said, were over. Now the United States must "be ready for preemptive action." He also said, "America has, and intends to keep, military strengths beyond challenge, thereby making the destabilizing arms races of other eras pointless." In short, the United States will establish, preserve, and make free use of an absolute military supremacy over every other nation on earth. As Richard Falk has observed in these pages, this policy discards several centuries of both American tradition and international law. Even Henry Kissinger has called the new approach "revolutionary," explaining that "regime change as a goal for military intervention challenges the international system established by the 1648 Treaty of Westphalia."

The Administration has been no more forthcoming on this specific plan than it has on the more general policies. There is no assurance so far that the public will be told whether or when the Administration has decided to attack Iraq before the bombs begin to fall. At an appearance before a gathering of troops at Fort Hood, Texas, Rumsfeld said, "The President has made no such decision that we should go into a war with Iraq." According to the *Times,* Rumsfeld added with a characteristic coy chuckle, "He's thinking about it."

A debate about the war, if the nation decides to have one, will be in vain if it does not address the wider revolution in policy of which the war is an expression. Will other nations claim for themselves the right of preemptive overthrow of hostile regimes? Can the proliferation of nuclear weapons actually be prevented by military force? Are negotiations and treaties worthless for this purpose? Will American superiority be so great that other arms races fade away? Will such action provoke the very military challenges, from terrorists and others, that it is meant to prevent? Should the United States aim at preserving military dominance over the earth for the indefinite future? Is such dominance possible? If it is possible, do the people of the United States want it? If the attempt is made, can the United States remain a democracy? Can the United States act as military guarantor of a world that rejects and hates its protector? George Bush is thinking about it. Are we?

The Case Against the War

MARCH 3, 2003

"All of us have heard this term 'preventive war' since the earliest days of Hitler. I recall that is about the first time I heard it. In this day and time . . . I don't believe there is such a thing; and, frankly, I wouldn't even listen to anyone seriously that came in and talked about such a thing."

—PRESIDENT DWIGHT EISENHOWER, 1953,
upon being presented with plans to wage
preventive war to disarm Stalin's Soviet Union

"Our position is that whatever grievances a nation may have, however objectionable it finds the status quo, aggressive warfare is an illegal means for settling those grievances or for altering those conditions."

—SUPREME COURT JUSTICE ROBERT JACKSON,
the American prosecutor at the Nuremberg trials,
in his opening statement to the tribunal

I. THE LOST WAR

In his poem "Fall 1961," written when the Cold War was at its zenith, Robert Lowell wrote:

All autumn, the chafe and jar
of nuclear war;
we have talked our extinction to death.

This autumn and winter, nuclear danger has returned, in a new form, accompanied by danger from the junior siblings in the mass destruction family, chemical and biological weapons. Now it is not a crisis between two superpowers but the planned war to overthrow the government of Iraq that, like a sentence of execution that has been passed but must go through its final appeals before being carried out, we have talked to death. (Has any war been so lengthily premeditated before it was launched?) Iraq, the United States insists, possesses some of these weapons. To take them away, the United States will overthrow the Iraqi government. No circumstance is more likely to provoke Iraq to use any forbidden weapons it has. In that event, the Bush Administration has repeatedly said, it will itself consider the use of nuclear weapons. Has there ever been a clearer or more present danger of the use of weapons of mass destruction?

While we were all talking and the danger was growing, strange to say, the war was being lost. For wars, let us recall, are not fought for their own sake but to achieve aims. Victory cannot be judged only by the outcome of battles. In the American Revolutionary War, for example, Edmund Burke, a leader of England's antiwar movement, said, "Our victories can only complete our ruin." Almost two centuries later, in Vietnam, the United States triumphed in almost every military engagement, yet lost the war. If the aim is lost, the war is lost, whatever happens on the battlefield. The novelty this time is that the defeat has preceded the inauguration of hostilities.

The aim of the Iraq war has never been only to disarm Iraq. George Bush set forth the full aim of his war policy in unmistakable terms on January 29, 2002, in his first State of the Union address. It was to stop the spread of weapons of mass destruction, not only in Iraq but everywhere in the world, through the use of military force. "We must," he said, "prevent the terrorists and regimes who seek chemical, biological or nuclear weapons from threatening the United States and the world." He underscored the scope of his ambition by singling out three countries—North Korea, Iran, and Iraq—for special mention, calling them an "axis of evil." Then came the ultimatum: "The United States of America will not permit the world's most dangerous regimes to threaten us with the world's most destructive weapons." Other possible war aims—to defeat Al Qaeda, to spread democracy—came and went in Administration pronouncements, but this one has remained constant. Stopping the spread of weapons of mass destruction is the reason for war given alike to the Security Council, whose inspectors are now searching for such weapons in Iraq, and to the American people, who were advised in the recent State of the Union address to fear "a day of horror like none we have ever known."

The means whereby the United States would stop the prohibited acquisitions were first set forth last June 1 in the President's speech to the graduating class at West Point. The United States would use force, and use it preemptively. "If we wait for threats to fully materialize, we will have waited too long," he said. For "the only path to safety is the path of action. And this nation will act." This strategy, too, has remained constant.

The Bush policy of using force to stop the spread of weapons of mass destruction met its Waterloo last October, when Assistant Secretary of State for East Asian and Pacific Affairs James Kelly was informed by Vice Foreign Minister Kang Sok Ju of

North Korea that his country has a perfect right to possess nuclear weapons. Shortly, Secretary of State Colin Powell stated, "We have to assume that they might have one or two. . . . that's what our intelligence community has been saying for some time." (Doubts, however, remain.) Next, North Korea went on to announce that it was terminating the Agreed Framework of 1994, under which it had shut down two reactors that produced plutonium. It ejected the UN inspectors who had been monitoring the agreement and then announced its withdrawal from the Nuclear Nonproliferation Treaty, under whose terms it was obligated to remain nuclear-weapon-free. Soon, America stated that North Korea might be moving fuel rods from existing reactors to its plutonium reprocessing plant, and that it possessed an untested missile capable of striking the western United States. "We will not permit . . . " had been Bush's words, but North Korea went ahead and apparently produced nuclear weapons anyway. The Administration now discovered that its policy of preemptively using overwhelming force had no application against a proliferator with a serious military capability, much less a nuclear power. North Korea's conventional capacity alone—it has an army of more than a million men and 11,000 artillery pieces capable of striking South Korea's capital, Seoul—imposed a very high cost; the addition of nuclear arms, in combination with missiles capable of striking not only South Korea but Japan, made it obviously prohibitive.

By any measure, totalitarian North Korea's possession of nuclear weapons is more dangerous than the mere possibility that Iraq is trying to develop them. The North Korean state, which is hard to distinguish from a cult, is also more repressive and disciplined than the Iraqi state, and has caused the death of more of its own people—through starvation. Yet in the weeks that followed the North Korean disclosure, the Administration, in a radical reversal of the President's earlier assessments, sought to argue that the opposite was true. Administration spokespersons soon declared that the North Korean situation was "not a crisis" and that its policy toward that country was to be one of "dialogue," leading to "a peaceful multilateral solution," including the possibility of renewed oil shipments. But if the acquisition by North Korea of nuclear arms was not a crisis, then there never had been any need to warn the world of the danger of nuclear proliferation, or to name an axis of evil, or to deliver an ultimatum to disarm it.

For the North Korean debacle represented not the failure of a good policy but exposure of the futility of one that was impracticable from the start. Nuclear proliferation, when considered as the global emergency that it is, has never been, is not now and never will be stoppable by military force; on the contrary, force can only exacerbate the problem. In announcing its policy, the United States appeared to have forgotten what proliferation is. It is not army divisions or tanks crossing borders; it is above all technical know-how passing from one mind to another. It cannot be stopped by B-2 bombers, or even Predator drones. The case of Iraq had indeed always been an anomaly in the wider picture of nonproliferation. In the 1991 Gulf War, the US-led coalition waged war to end Iraq's occupation of Kuwait. In the process it stumbled on Saddam Hussein's program for building weapons of mass destruction, and made use of the defeat to impose on him the new obligation to end the program. A war fought for one purpose led to peace terms serving another. It was a historical chain of events unlikely ever to be repeated, and offered no model for dealing with proliferation.

The lesson so far? Exactly the opposite of the intended one: If you want to avoid "regime change" by the United States, build a nuclear arsenal—but be sure to do it quietly and fast. As Mohamed El Baradei, the director general of the International Atomic Energy Agency, has said, the United States seems to want to teach the world that "if you really want to defend yourself, develop nuclear weapons, because then you get negotiations, and not military action."

Although the third of the "axis" countries presents no immediate crisis, events there also illustrate the bankruptcy of the Bush policy. With the help of Russia, Iran is building nuclear reactors that are widely believed to double as a nuclear weapons program. American threats against Iraq have failed to dissuade Iran—or for that matter, its supplier, Russia—from proceeding. Just this week, Iran announced that it had begun to mine uranium on its own soil. Iran's path to acquiring nuclear arms, should it decide to go ahead, is clear. "Regime change" by American military action in that half-authoritarian, half-democratic country is a formula for disaster. Whatever the response of the Iraqi people might be to an American invasion, there is little question that in Iran hard-liners and democrats alike would mount bitter, protracted resistance. Nor is there evidence that democratization in Iraq, even in the unlikely event that it should succeed, would be a sure path to denuclearization. The world's first nuclear power, after all, was a democracy, and of nine nuclear powers now in the world, six—the United States, England, France, India, Israel, and Russia—are also democracies. Iran, within striking range of Israel, lives in an increasingly nuclearized neighborhood. In these circumstances, would the Iranian people be any more likely to rebel against nuclearization than the Indian people did—or more, for that matter, than the American people have done? And if a democratic Iran obtained the bomb, would preemption or regime change then be an option for the United States?

The collapse of the overall Bush policy has one more element that may be even more significant than the appearance of North Korea's arsenal or Iran's apparently unstoppable discreet march to obtaining the bomb. It has turned out that the supplier of essential information and technology for North Korea's uranium program was America's faithful ally in the war on terrorism, Pakistan, which received missile technology from Korea in return. The "father" of Pakistan's bomb, Ayub Qadeer Khan, has visited North Korea thirteen times. This is the same Pakistan whose nuclear scientist Sultan Bashiruddin Mahood paid a visit to Osama bin Laden in Afghanistan a few months before September 11, and whose nuclear establishment even today is riddled with Islamic fundamentalists. The BBC has reported that the Al Qaeda network succeeded at one time in building a "dirty bomb" (which may account for Osama bin Laden's claim that he possesses nuclear weapons), and Pakistan is the likeliest source for the materials involved, although Russia is also a candidate. Pakistan, in short, has proved itself to be the world's most dangerous proliferator, having recently acquired nuclear weapons itself and passed on nuclear technology to a state and, possibly, to a terrorist group.

Indeed, an objective ranking of nuclear proliferators in order of menace would place Pakistan (a possessor of the bomb that also purveys the technology to others) first on the list, North Korea second (it peddles missiles but not, so far, bomb technology), Iran (a country of growing political and military power with an active nuclear program) third, and Iraq (a country of shrinking military power that probably has no nuclear program and is currently under international sanctions and an unprecedented inspection regime of indefinite duration) fourth. (Russia, possessor of 150 tons of poorly guarded plutonium, also belongs somewhere on this list.) The Bush Administration ranks them, of course, in exactly the reverse order, placing Iraq, which it plans to attack, first, and Pakistan, which it befriends and coddles, nowhere on the list. It will not be possible, however, to right this pyramid. The reason it is upside down is that it was unworkable right side up. Iraq is being attacked not because it is the worst proliferator but because it is the weakest.

The *reductio ad absurdum* of the failed American war policy was illustrated by a recent column in the *Washington Post* by the superhawk Charles Krauthammer. Krauthammer wants nothing to do with soft measures; yet he, too, can see that the cost of using force against North Korea would be prohibitive: "Militarily, we are not even in position to bluff." He rightly understands, too, that in the climate created by pending war in Iraq, "dialogue" is scarcely likely to succeed. He has therefore come up with a new idea. He identifies China as the solution. China must twist the arm of its Communist ally North Korea. "If China and South Korea were to cut off North Korea, it could not survive," he observes. But to make China do so, the United States must twist China's arm. How? By encouraging Japan to build nuclear weapons. For "if our nightmare is a nuclear North Korea, China's is a nuclear Japan." It irks Krauthammer that the United States alone has to face up to the North Korean threat. Why shouldn't China shoulder some of the burden? He wants to "share the nightmares." Indeed. He wants to stop nuclear proliferation with more nuclear proliferation. Here the nuclear age comes full circle. The only nation ever to use the bomb is to push the nation on which it dropped it to build the bomb and threaten others.

As a recommendation for policy, Krauthammer's suggestion is Strangelovian, but if it were considered as a prediction it would be sound. Nuclear armament by North Korea really will tempt neighboring nations—not only Japan but South Korea and Taiwan—to acquire nuclear weapons. (Japan has an abundant supply of plutonium and all the other technology necessary, and both South Korea and Taiwan have had nuclear programs but were persuaded by the United States to drop them.) In a little-noticed comment, Japan's foreign minister has already stated that the nuclearization of North Korea would justify a preemptive strike against it by Japan. Thus has the Bush plan to stop proliferation already become a powerful force promoting it. The policy of preemptive war has led to preemptive defeat.

General Groves Redux

Radical as the Bush Administration policy is, the idea behind it is not new. Two months after the bombing of Hiroshima and Nagasaki, Gen. Leslie Groves, the Pentagon overseer of the

Manhattan Project, expressed his views on controlling nuclear proliferation. He said:

> If we were truly realistic instead of idealistic, as we appear to be [*sic*], we would not permit any foreign power with which we are not firmly allied, and in which we do not have absolute confidence, to make or possess atomic weapons. If such a country started to make atomic weapons we would destroy its capacity to make them before it has progressed far enough to threaten us.

The proposal was never seriously considered by President Truman and, until now, has been rejected by every subsequent President. Eisenhower's views of preventive war are given in the epigraph at the beginning of this article. In 1961, during the Berlin crisis, a few of Kennedy's advisers made the surprising discovery that Russia's nuclear forces were far weaker and more vulnerable than anyone had thought. They proposed a preventive strike. Ted Sorensen, the chief White House counsel and speechwriter, was told of the plan. He shouted, "You're crazy! We shouldn't let guys like you around here." It never came to the attention of the President.

How has it happened that President Bush has revived and implemented this long-buried, long-rejected idea? We know the answer. The portal was September 11. The theme of the "war on terror" was from the start to strike preemptively with military force. Piece by piece, a bridge from the aim of catching Osama bin Laden to the aim of stopping proliferation on a global basis was built. First came the idea of holding whole regimes accountable in the war on terror; then the idea of "regime change" (beginning with Afghanistan), then preemption, then the broader claim of American global dominance. Gradually, the most important issue of the age—the rising danger from weapons of mass destruction—was subsumed as a sort of codicil to the war on terror. When the process was finished, the result was the Groves plan writ large—a reckless and impracticable idea when it was conceived, when only one hostile nuclear power (the Soviet Union) was in prospect, and a worse one today in our world of nine nuclear powers (if you count North Korea) and many scores of nuclear-capable ones.

The Administration now hints, however, that although its overall nonproliferation policy might be in trouble, the forcible disarmament of Iraq still makes sense on its own terms. Bush now claims that "different threats require different strategies"— apparently forgetting that the Iraq policy was announced with great fanfare in the context of a global policy of preserving the world from weapons of mass destruction. The mainstream argument, shared by many doubters as well as supporters of the war, is that if Iraq is shown to possess weapons of mass destruction, its regime must be attacked and destroyed. Thus the only question is whether Iraq has the weapons. A team of "realist" analysts, organized by Stephen Walt of Harvard's John F. Kennedy School of Government and John Mearsheimer of the University of Chicago, have given a convincing response: They are prepared to live with a nuclear-armed Iraq. "The United States can contain a nuclear Iraq," they write. They argue that Hussein belongs, like his idol Stalin, in the class of rational monsters. The idea that he is not deterrable is "almost certainly wrong."

He wants power; he knows that to engage again in aggression is to insure his overthrow and likely his personal extinction. The record of his wars—against Iran, against Kuwait—shows him to be brutal but calculating. He is sixty-five years old. Time will solve the problem, as it did with the Soviet Union.

What is of most desperately immediate concern, however, is that America's preemptive war will lead directly to the use of the weapons whose mere possession the war is supposed to prevent. In the debate over the inspections now going on in Iraq, it sometimes seems to be forgotten that Iraq either does possess weapons of mass destruction (as Colin Powell has just asserted at the UN) or does not possess them, and that each alternative has consequences that go far beyond the decision whether or not to go to war. If Iraq does not have these weapons, then the war will be an unnecessary, wholly avoidable slaughter. If Iraq does have the weapons, then there is a likelihood that it will use them. Why else would Saddam Hussein, having created them, bring on the destruction of his regime and his personal extinction by hiding them from the UN inspectors? And if in fact he does use them, then the United States, as it has made clear, will consider using nuclear weapons in retaliation. Powell has asserted that Saddam has recently given his forces fresh orders to use chemical weapons. Against whom? In what circumstances? Is it possible that this outcome—a Hitlerian finale—is what Hussein seeks? Could it be his plan, if cornered, to provoke the United States into the first use of nuclear weapons since Nagasaki?

We cannot know, but we do know that White House Chief of Staff Andrew Card has stated that if Iraq uses weapons of mass destruction against American troops "the United States will use whatever means necessary to protect us and the world from a holocaust"—"whatever means" being diplomatese for nuclear attack. The *Washington Times* has revealed that National Security Presidential Directive 17, issued secretly on September 14 of last year, says in plain English what Card expressed obliquely. It reads, "The United States will continue to make clear that it reserves the right to respond with over-whelming force—including potentially nuclear weapons—to the use of [weapons of mass destruction] against the United States, our forces abroad, and friends and allies." Israel has also used diplomatese to make known its readiness to retaliate with nuclear weapons if attacked by Iraq. Condoleezza Rice has threatened the Iraqi people with genocide: If Iraq uses weapons of mass destruction, she says, it knows it will bring "national obliteration." (Threats of genocide are flying thick and fast around the world these days. In January, Indian Defense Minister George Fernandes threatened that if Pakistan launched a nuclear attack on India—as Pakistan's President Pervez Musharraf has threatened to do if India invades Pakistan—then "there will be no Pakistan left when we have responded.") William Arkin writes in the *Los Angeles Times* that the United States is "drafting contingency plans for the use of nuclear weapons." STRATCOM—the successor to the Strategic Air Command—has been ordered to consider ways in which nuclear weapons can be used preemptively, either to destroy underground facilities or to respond to the use or threats of use of weapons of mass destruction against the United States or its forces.

Oil and Democracy

Other critics of the war have concluded from the disparity in America's treatment of Iraq and North Korea that the Administration's aim is not to deal with weapons of mass destruction at all but to seize Iraq's oil, which amounts to some 10 percent of the world's known reserves. The very fact that the Bush Administration refuses even to discuss the oil question (the war "has nothing to do with oil," Defense Secretary Donald Rumsfeld has said) suggests that the influence of oil is moving powerfully in the background. One is tempted to respond to Rumsfeld that if the Administration is not thinking about the consequences of a war for the global oil regime, it is culpably neglecting the security interests of the United States. However, there is in fact no contradiction between the goals of disarming Iraq and seizing its oil. Both fit neatly into the larger scheme of American global dominance.

Still other critics place the emphasis not on oil but on political reform of Iraq and even the entire Middle East. Thomas Friedman of the *New York Times* is prepared to support Hussein's overthrow, but only if we "do it right"—which is to say that we devote the "time and effort" to creating "a self-sustaining, progressive, accountable Arab government" in Iraq. And this delightful government (can we have one at home, too, please?), in turn, must become "a progressive model for the whole region." "Our kids" can grow up in "a safer world" only "if we help put Iraq on a more progressive path and stimulate some real change in an Arab world that is badly in need of reform." Fouad Ajami, of Johns Hopkins University, likewise wants the United

States to get over its "dread of nation-building" and spearhead "a reformist project that seeks to modernize and transform the Arab landscape," now mired in "retrogression and political decay." Michael Ignatieff, director of the Carr Center for Human Rights at Harvard, is also of the "do it right" school. His starting point, however, is the need to disarm Iraq. In his essay in *The New York Times Magazine* "The American Empire: The Burden," he begins by noting that if Saddam Hussein is permitted to have weapons of mass destruction, he will have a "capacity to intimidate and deter others, including the United States." Being deterred in a region of interest is evidently unacceptable for an imperial power, and forces it to remove the offending regime. Yet if the regime is to be removed, a larger imperial agenda becomes inescapable. By this reasoning Ignatieff arrives at the same destination as Friedman and Ajami: The United States must mount "an imperial operation that would commit a reluctant republic to become the guarantor of peace, stability, democratization, and oil supplies in a combustible region of Islamic peoples stretching from Egypt to Afghanistan." We arrive at a new formula that has no precedent for dealing with nuclear danger: nonproliferation by forced democratization. Ignatieff acknowledges that a republic that turns into an empire risks "endangering its identity as a free people"—thus menacing democracy at home by trying to force it on others abroad. Nevertheless, he wants the United States to take on "the burden of empire."

The Bush Administration, however, has given little encouragement to the evangelists of armed democratization. Notoriously, it has kept silent regarding its plans for postwar Iraq and its neighbors. But if its actions in the "war on terror" are any guide, democracy will not be required of Washington's imperial dependencies. The Bush Administration has been perfectly happy, for example, to extend its cooperation to such allies as totalitarian Turkmenistan and authoritarian Uzbekistan and Kazakhstan—not to speak of such longstanding autocratic allies of the United States as Egypt and Saudi Arabia. The United States has in fact never insisted on democracy as a condition for good relations with other countries. Its practice during the Cold War probably offers as accurate a guide to the future as any. The United States was pleased to have democratic allies, including most of the countries of Europe, but was also ready when needed to install or prop up such brutal, repressive regimes as (to mention only a few) that of Reza Pahlavi in Iran, Saddam Hussein in Iraq (until he invaded Kuwait), Mobutu Sese Seko in Zaire (now Congo), Fulgencio Batista in Cuba, Park Chung Hee in South Korea, a succession of civilian and military dictators in South Vietnam, Lon Nol in Cambodia, Suharto in Indonesia, Ferdinand Marcos in the Philippines, the colonels' junta in Greece, Francisco Franco in Spain and a long list of military dictators in Argentina, Chile, Brazil, Uruguay, Guatemala, El Salvador, and Nicaragua.

The Administration has in any case made its broader conception of democracy clear in its actions both at home and abroad. In this conception, the Administration decides and others are permitted to express their agreement. (Or else they become, as the President has said threateningly to the UN, "irrelevant"— although it's hard to imagine what it means to say that the assembled representatives of the peoples of the earth are irrelevant. Irrelevant to what?) Just as the Administration welcomed a Congressional expression of support for the Bush war policy but denied it the power to stop the war if that were to be its choice, and just as the Administration "welcomes" a vote for war in NATO and the UN but denies either NATO or the UN the right to prevent unilateral American action, so we can expect that the people of Iraq or any other country the United States might "democratize" would be "free" to support but not to oppose American policy. (Imagine, for example, that the people of Iraq were to vote, as so many other free peoples, including the American people, have done before them, to build nuclear arsenals—perhaps on the ground that their enemy Israel already has them and Iran was building them. Would the Bush Administration accept their decision?)

We do not have to wait for war in Iraq, however, to consider the likely impact of Washington's new policies on democracy's global fortunes. The question has already arisen in the period of preparation for war. The Bush Administration has not forced the world to read between the lines to discover its position. It proposes for the world at large the same two-tier system that it proposes for the decision to go to war and for the possession of weapons of mass destruction: It lays claim to absolute military hegemony over the earth. "America has, and intends to keep, military strengths beyond challenge, thereby making the destabilizing arms races of other eras pointless, and limiting rivalries to trade and other pursuits of peace," the President said in his speech at West Point. The United States alone will be the custodian of military power; others must turn to humbler pursuits. The sword will rule, and the United States will hold the sword. As the Yale historian John Lewis Gaddis has pointed out, the policies of unilateral preemption, overthrow of governments, and overall military supremacy form an integral package (the seizure of Middle Eastern oilfields, though officially denied as a motive, also fits in). These elements are the foundations of the imperial system that Ignatieff and others have delineated.

However, empire is incompatible with democracy, whether at home or abroad. Democracy is founded on the rule of law, empire on the rule of force. Democracy is a system of self-determination, empire a system of military conquest. The fault lines are already clear, and growing wider every day. By every measure, public opinion in the world—its democratic will—is opposed to over-throwing the government of Iraq by force. But why, someone might ask, does this matter? How many divisions do these people have, as Stalin once asked of the Pope? The answer, to the extent that the world really is democratic, is: quite a few. In a series of elections—in Germany, in South Korea, in Turkey—an antiwar position helped bring the winner to power. In divided Korea, American policy may be on its way to producing an unexpected union of South and North—against the United States. Each of these setbacks is a critical defeat for the putative American empire. In January, the prime ministers of eight countries—Italy, Britain, Spain, Portugal, Denmark, Poland, the Czech Republic, and Hungary—signed a letter thanking the United States for its leadership on the Iraq issue; but in every one of those countries a majority of the public opposed a war without UN approval. The editors of *Time*'s European edition asked its readers which nation posed the greatest threat to world peace. Of the 268,000 who responded, 8 percent answered that it was North Korea, 9 percent Iraq, and 83 percent said the United States. Britain's

Prime Minister Tony Blair is prepared to participate in the war without UN support, but some 70 percent of his people oppose his position. The government of Australia is sending troops to assist in the war effort, but 92 percent of the Australian public opposes war unsanctioned by the UN. Gaddis rightly comments that empires succeed to the extent that peoples under their rule welcome and share the values of the imperial power. The above election results and poll figures suggest that no such approval is so far evident for America's global pretensions. The American "coalition" for war is an alliance of governments arrayed in opposition to their own peoples.

In a defeat parallel to—and greater than—the military defeat before the fact in the field of proliferation, the American empire is thus suffering deep and possibly irreversible political losses. Democracy is the right of peoples to make decisions. Right now, the peoples of the earth are deciding against America's plans for the world. Democracy, too, has preemptive resources, setting up impassable roadblocks at the first signs of tyranny. The UN Security Council is balking. The United States' most important alliance—NATO—is cracking. Is the American empire collapsing before it even quite comes into existence? Such a judgment is premature, but if the mere approach to war has done the damage we already see to America's reputation and power, we can only imagine what the consequences of actual war will be.

II. The Atomic Archipelago

The Administration has embarked on a nonproliferation policy that has already proved as self-defeating in its own terms as it is likely to be disastrous for the United States and the world. Nevertheless, it would be a fatal mistake for those of us who oppose the war to dismiss the concerns that the Administration has raised. By insisting that the world confront the proliferation of weapons of mass destruction, President Bush has raised the right question—or, at any rate, one part of the right question—for our time, even as he has given a calamitously misguided answer. Even if it were true—and we won't really know until some equivalent of the Pentagon Papers for our period is released—that his Administration has been using the threat of mass destruction as a cover for an oil grab, the issue of proliferation must be placed at the center of our concerns. For example, even as we argue that containment of Iraq makes more sense than war, we must be clear-eyed in acknowledging that Iraq's acquisition of nuclear weapons or other weapons of mass destruction would be a disaster—just as we must recognize that the nuclearization of South Asia and of North Korea have been disasters, greatly increasing the likelihood of nuclear war in the near future. These events, full of peril in themselves, are points on a curve of proliferation that leads to what can only be described as nuclear anarchy.

For a global policy that, unlike the Bush policies, actually will stop—and reverse—proliferation of all weapons of mass destruction is indeed a necessity for a sane, livable twenty-first century. But if we are to tackle the problem wisely, we must step back from the current crisis long enough to carefully analyze the origins and character of the danger. It did not appear on September 11. It appeared, in fact, on July 16, 1945, when the United States detonated the first atomic bomb near Alamogordo, New Mexico.

What is proliferation? It is the acquisition of nuclear weapons by a country that did not have them before. The first act of proliferation was the Manhattan Project in the United States. (In what follows, I will speak of nuclear proliferation, but the principles underlying it also underlie the proliferation of chemical and biological weapons.) Perhaps someone might object that the arrival of the first individual of a species is not yet proliferation—a word that suggests the multiplication of an already existing thing. However, in one critical respect, at least, the development of the bomb by the United States still fits the definition. The record shows that President Franklin Roosevelt decided to build the bomb because he feared that Hitler would get it first, with decisive consequences in the forthcoming war. In October 1939, when the businessman Alexander Sachs brought Roosevelt a letter from Albert Einstein warning that an atomic bomb was possible and that Germany might acquire one, Roosevelt commented, "Alex, what you are after is to see that the Nazis don't blow us up." As we know now, Hitler did have an atomic project, but it never came close to producing a bomb. But as with so many matters in nuclear strategy, appearances were more important than the realities (which were then unknowable to the United States). Before there was the bomb, there was the fear of the bomb. Hitler's phantom arsenal inspired the real American one. And so even before nuclear weapons existed, they were proliferating. This sequence is important because it reveals a basic rule that has driven nuclear proliferation ever since: Nations acquire nuclear arsenals above all because they fear the nuclear arsenals of others.

But fear—soon properly renamed terror in the context of

nuclear strategy—is of course also the essence of the prime strategic doctrine of the nuclear age, deterrence, which establishes a balance of terror. Threats of the destruction of nations—of genocide—have always been the coinage of this realm. From the beginning of the nuclear age—indeed, even before the beginning, when the atomic bomb was only a gleam in Roosevelt's eye—deterrence and proliferation have in fact been inextricable. Just as the United States made the bomb because it feared Hitler would get it, the Soviet Union built the bomb because the United States already had it. Stalin's instructions to his scientists shortly after Hiroshima were, "A single demand of you, comrades: Provide us with atomic weapons in the shortest possible time. You know that Hiroshima has shaken the whole world. The equilibrium has been destroyed. Provide the bomb—it will remove a great danger from us." England and France, like the United States, were responding to the Soviet threat; China was responding to the threat from all of the above; India was responding to China; Pakistan was responding to India; and North Korea (with Pakistan's help) was responding to the United States. Nations proliferate in order to deter. We can state: Deterrence equals proliferation, for deterrence both causes proliferation and is the fruit of it. This has been the lesson, indeed, that the United States has taught the world in every major statement, tactic, strategy, and action it has taken in the nuclear age. And the world—if it even needed the lesson—has learned well. It is therefore hardly surprising that the call to nonproliferation falls on deaf ears when it is preached by possessors—all of whom were of course proliferators at one time or another.

The sources of nuclear danger, present and future, are perhaps best visualized as a coral reef that is constantly growing in all directions under the sea and then, here and there, breaks the surface to form islands, which we can collectively call the atomic archipelago. The islands of the archipelago may seem to be independent of one another, but anyone who looks below the surface will find that they are closely connected. The atomic archipelago indeed has strong similarities to its namesake, the gulag archipelago. Once established, both feed on themselves, expanding from within by their own energy and momentum. Both are founded upon a capacity to kill millions of people. Both act on the world around them by radiating terror.

India and the Bomb: The Proliferator's View

India's path to nuclear armament, recounted in George Perkovich's masterful, definitive India's Nuclear Bomb, offers essential lessons in the steps by which the archipelago has grown and is likely to grow in the future. India has maintained a nuclear program almost since its independence, in 1947. Although supposedly built for peaceful uses, the program was actually, if mostly secretly, designed to keep the weapons option open. But it was not until shortly after China tested a bomb in 1964 that India embarked on a concerted nuclear weapons program, which bore fruit in 1974, when India tested a bomb for "peaceful" purposes. Yet India still held back from introducing nuclear weapons into its military forces. Meanwhile, Pakistan, helped by China, was working hard to obtain the bomb. In May of 1998, India conducted five nuclear tests. Pakistan responded with at least five, and both nations promptly declared themselves nuclear powers and soon were engaged in a major nuclear confrontation over the disputed territory of Kashmir.

Indian Foreign Minister Jaswant Singh has explained the reasons for India's decision in an article in Foreign Affairs. India looked out upon the world and saw what he calls a "nuclear paradigm" in operation. He liked what he saw. He writes, "Why admonish India after the fact for not falling in line behind a new international agenda of discriminatory nonproliferation pursued largely due to the internal agendas or political debates of the nuclear club? If deterrence works in the West—as it so obviously appears to, since Western nations insist on continuing to possess nuclear weapons—by what reasoning will it not work in India?" To deprive India of these benefits would be "nuclear apartheid"—a continuation of the imperialism that had been overthrown in the titanic anticolonial struggles of the twentieth century. The Nuclear Nonproliferation Treaty, under which 183 nations have agreed to forgo nuclear arms, and five who have them (the United States, England, France, Russia and China) have agreed to reduce theirs until they are gone, had many successes, but in India's backyard, where China had nuclear arms and Pakistan was developing them, nuclear danger was growing. Some have charged that the Indian government conducted the 1998 tests for political rather than strategic reasons—that is, out of a desire for pure "prestige," not strategic necessity. But the two explanations are in fact complementary. It is only because the public, which observes that all the great powers possess nuclear arsenals, agrees that they are a strategic necessity that it finds them prestigious and politically rewards governments that acquire them. Prestige is merely the political face of the general consensus, ingrained in strategy, that countries lacking nuclear weapons are helpless—"eunuchs," as one Indian politician said—in a nuclear-armed world.

Curiously, the unlimited extension in 1995 of the NPT, to which India was not a signatory, pushed India to act. From Singh's point of view, the extension made the nuclear double standard it embodied permanent. "What India did in May [1998] was to assert that it is impossible to have two standards for national security—one based on nuclear deterrence and the other outside of it." If the world was to be divided into two classes of countries, India preferred to be in the first class.

As Singh's account makes clear, India was inspired to act not merely by the hypocrisy of great powers delivering sermons on the virtues of nuclear disarmament while sitting atop mountains of nuclear arms—galling as that might be. He believed that India, with nuclear-armed China and nuclearizing Pakistan for neighbors, was living in an increasingly "dangerous neighborhood." The most powerful tie that paradoxically binds proliferator to deterrer in their minuet of genocidal hostility is not mere imitation but the compulsion to respond to the nuclear terror projected by others. The preacher against lust who turns out to take prostitutes to a motel after the sermon sets a bad example but does not compel his parishioners to follow suit. The preacher against nuclear weapons in a nation whose silos are packed with them does, however, compel other nations to follow his example, for his nuclear terror reaches and crosses their borders. The United States terrorizes Russia (and vice versa); both terrorize China; China terrorizes India; the United States terrorizes North Korea; North Korea terrorizes Japan; and so forth, forming a web of terror whose further extensions (Israel terrorizes . . . Iran? Egypt?

Syria? Libya?) will be the avenues of future proliferation. It is thanks to this web that every nuclear arsenal in the world is tied, directly or indirectly, to every other, rendering any partial approach to the problem extremely difficult, if not impossible.

The devotion of nations to their nuclear arsenals has only been strengthened by the hegemonic ambition of the United States. Hitherto, the nuclear double standard lacked a context—it was a sort of anomaly of the international order, a seeming leftover from the Cold War, perhaps soon to be liquidated. America's imperial ambition gives it a context. In a multilateral, democratic vision of international affairs, it is impossible to explain why one small group of nations should be entitled to protect itself with weapons of mass destruction while all others must do without them. But in an imperial order, the reason is perfectly obvious. If the imperium is to pacify the world, it must possess overwhelming force, the currency of imperial power. Equally obviously, the nations to be pacified must not. Double standards—regarding not only nuclear weapons but conventional weapons, economic advantage, use of natural resources—are indeed the very stuff of which empires are made. For empire is to the world what dictatorship is to a country. That's why the suppression of proliferation—a new imperial vocation—must be the first order of business for a nation aspiring to this exalted role.

India's Bomb: The Possessor's View

It's equally enlightening to look at India's proliferation from the point of view of a nuclear possessor, the United States. Nuclear arsenals are endowed with a magical quality. As soon as a nation obtains one it becomes invisible to the possessor. Nuclear danger then seems to emanate only from proliferation—that is, from newcomers to the nuclear club, while the dangers that emanate from one's own arsenal disappear from sight. Gen. Tommy Franks, designated as commander of the Iraq war, recently commented, "The sight of the first mushroom cloud on one of the major population centers on this planet is something that most nations on this planet are willing to go a long ways out of the way to prevent." His forgetfulness of Hiroshima and Nagasaki might seem nothing more than a slip of the tongue if it did not represent a pervasive and deeply ingrained attitude in the United States. Another revealing incident was Secretary of State Powell's comment that North Korea, by seeking nuclear weapons, was arming itself with "fool's gold." But the military establishment that Powell once led is of course stuffed to bursting with this fool's gold. Another example of the same habit of mind (I have chosen American examples, but the blindness afflicts all nuclear powers) was provided by some comments of President Bill Clinton shortly after India's tests of 1998. He said, "To think that you have to manifest your greatness by behavior that recalls the very worst events of the twentieth century on the edge of the twenty-first century, when everybody else is trying to leave the nuclear age behind, is just wrong. And they [the Indians] clearly don't need it to maintain their security." Wise words, but ones contradicted by more than a half-century of the nuclear policies, including the current ones, of the nation he led.

The reactions of some of America's most prominent thinkers on the nuclear question to India's proliferation were also instructive. Almost immediately, their belief in the virtues of nuclear arms began to surface through the antiproliferation rhetoric. Henry Kissinger, for instance, judiciously mocked Clinton's "unique insight into the nature of greatness in the twenty-first century . . . the dubious proposition that all other nations are trying to leave the nuclear world behind," and "the completely unsupported proposition that countries with threatening nuclear neighbors do not need nuclear weapons to assure their security." Kissinger, more consistent than Clinton, found India's and Pakistan's tests "equally reasonable." He thought Washington's best course was to help its new nuclear-armed friends achieve "stable mutual deterrence," and "give stabilizing reassurances about their conventional security." Kissinger even saw a silver lining for American interests in the hope that nuclear-armed India would help the United States "contain China" (the very China to which Krauthammer now turns to disarm North Korea). It was Kissinger's view, not Clinton's, that soon prevailed. America's own love affair with the bomb asserted itself. At first, the United States imposed sanctions on both countries, but soon they were lifted. In December of 2000 President Clinton paid the first visit by an American President to India since 1978, confirming that becoming a nuclear power was indeed the path to international prestige. The United States now has growing programs of military cooperation with both countries.

Kissinger merely adjusted to the irreversible fait accompli of South Asian proliferation, as a realist should. He saw the tension between America's love of its own nuclear bombs and its hatred of others', and understood the problems this might cause for America's own arsenal. Could nonproliferation get out of control? Might it reach America's shores? "The administration is right to resist nuclear proliferation," he wrote, "but it must not, in the process, disarm the country psychologically."

III. One Will for One World

War in Iraq has not yet begun, but its most important lesson, taught also by the long history of proliferation, including the Indian chapter just discussed, is already plain: The time is long gone—if it ever existed—when any major element of the danger of weapons of mass destruction, including above all nuclear danger, can be addressed realistically without taking into account the whole dilemma. When we look at the story of proliferation, whether from the point of view of the haves or the have-nots, what emerges is that for practical purposes any distinction that once might have existed (and even then only in appearance, not in reality) between possessors and proliferators has now been erased. A rose is a rose is a rose, anthrax is anthrax is anthrax, a thermonuclear weapon is a thermonuclear weapon is a thermonuclear weapon. The world's prospective nuclear arsenals cannot be dealt with without attending to its existing ones. As long as some countries insist on having any of these, others will try to get them. Until this axiom is understood, neither "dialogue" nor war can succeed. In Perkovich's words, after immersing himself in the history of India's bomb, "the grandest illusion of the nuclear age is that a handful of states possessing nuclear weapons can secure themselves and the world indefinitely against the dangers of nuclear proliferation *without* placing a higher priority on simultaneously striving to eliminate their own nuclear weapons."

The days of the double standard are over. We cannot preserve it and we should not want to. The struggle to maintain it by force, anachronistically represented by Bush's proposed war on Iraq, in which the United States threatens preemptive use of nuclear weapons to stop another country merely from getting them, can only worsen the global problem it seeks to solve. One way or another, the world is on its way to a single standard. Only two in the long run are available: universal permission to possess weapons of mass destruction or their universal prohibition. The first is a path to global nightmare, the second to safety and a normal existence. Nations that already possess nuclear weapons must recognize that nuclear danger begins with them. The shield of invisibility must be pierced. The web of terror that binds every nuclear arsenal to every other—and also to every arsenal of chemical or biological weapons—must be acknowledged.

If preemptive military force leads to catastrophe and deterrence is at best a stopgap, then what is the answer? In 1945, the great Danish nuclear physicist Niels Bohr said simply, in words whose truth has been confirmed by fifty-eight years of experience of the nuclear age, "We are in a completely new situation that cannot be resolved by war." In a formulation only slightly more complex than Bohr's, Einstein said in 1947, "This basic power of the universe cannot be fitted into the outdated concept of narrow nationalisms. For there is no secret and there is no defense; there is no possibility of control except through the aroused understanding and insistence of the peoples of the world." Both men, whose work in fundamental physics had perhaps done more than that of any other two scientists to make the bomb possible, favored the abolition of nuclear arms by binding international agreement. That idea, also favored by many of the scientists of the Manhattan Project, bore fruit in a plan for the abolition of nuclear arms and international control of all nuclear technology put forward by President Truman's representative Bernard Baruch in June 1946. But the time was not ripe. The Cold War was already brewing, and the Soviet Union, determined to build its own bomb, said no, then put forward a plan that the United States turned down. In 1949 the Soviet Union conducted its first atomic test, and the nuclear arms race ensued.

For the short term, the inspections in Iraq should continue. If inspections fail, then containment will do as a second line of defense. But in the long term, the true alternative to preemptive war against Iraq, war one day against North Korea, war against an unknowable number of other possible proliferators, is to bring Bohr and Einstein's proposal up to date. A revival of worldwide disarmament negotiations must be the means, the abolition of all weapons of mass destruction the end. That idea has long been in eclipse, and today it lies outside the mainstream of political opinion. Unfortunately, historical reality is no respecter of conventional wisdom and often requires it to change course if calamity is to be avoided. But fortunately it is one element of the genius of democracy—and of US democracy in particular—that encrusted orthodoxy can be challenged and overthrown by popular pressure. The movement *against* the war in Iraq should also become a movement for something, and that something should be a return to the long-neglected path to abolition of all weapons of mass destruction. Only by offering a solution to the problem that the war claims to solve but does not can this war and others be stopped.

The passage of time since the failure in 1946 has also provided us with some advantages. No insuperable ideological division divides the nuclear powers (with the possible exception, now, of North Korea), as the Cold War did. Their substantial unity and agreement in this area can be imagined. Every other nonnuclear nation but one (the eccentric holdout is Cuba) already has agreed under the terms of the Nuclear Nonproliferation Treaty to do without nuclear weapons. Biological and chemical weapons have been banned by international conventions (although the conventions are weak, as they lack serious inspection and enforcement provisions).

The inspected and enforced elimination of weapons of mass destruction is a goal that in its very nature must take time, and adequate time—perhaps a decade, or even more—can be allowed. But the decision to embrace the goal should not wait. It should be seen not as a distant dream that may or may not be realized once a host of other unlikely prerequisites have been met but as a powerful instrument to be used immediately to halt all forms of proliferation and inspire arms reductions in the present. There can be no successful nonproliferation policy that is not backed by the concerted will of the international community. As long as the double standard is in effect, that will cannot be created. Do we need more evidence than the world's disarray today in the face of Iraq's record of proliferation? Today's world, to paraphrase Lincoln, is a house divided, half nuclear-armed, half nuclear-weapons-free. A commitment to the elimination of weapons of mass destruction would heal the world's broken will, and is the only means available for doing so. Great powers that were getting out of the mass destruction business would have very short patience with nations, such as Iraq or North Korea, getting into that business. The Security Council would act as one. The smaller powers that had never made their pact with the devil in the first place would be at the great powers' side. Any proliferator would face the implacable resolve of all nations to persuade it or force it to reverse its course.

Let us try to imagine it: one human species on its one earth exercising one will to defeat forever a threat to its one collective existence. Could any nation stand against it? Without this commitment, the international community—if I may express it thus—is like a nuclear reactor from which the fuel rods have been withdrawn. Making the commitment would be to insert the rods, to start up the chain reaction. The chain reaction would be the democratic activity of peoples demanding action from the governments to secure their survival. True democracy is indispensable to disarmament, and vice versa. This is the power—not the power of cruise missiles and B-52s—that can release humanity from its peril. The price demanded of us for freedom from the danger of weapons of mass destruction is to relinquish our own.

The Will of the World

MARCH 10, 2003

FEBRUARY 15, 2003, the day ten million or so people in hundreds of cities on every continent demonstrated against war in Iraq, will go down in history as the first time that the people of the world expressed their clear and concerted will in regard to a pressing global issue. Never before—not during the Vietnam War, not during the antinuclear demonstrations of the early 1980s—had they made known their will so forcefully by all the means at their disposal. On that day, history may one day record, global democracy was born.

Several elements unexpectedly (isn't the spontaneous expression of a people's will always unexpected?) snapped into place, like the components on an assembly line. One was a concatenation of opinion polls, showing that in the vast majority of the countries in which people were free to express their views, they opposed war against Iraq unless sanctioned by the United Nations. In every European country, a majority of the public supports this view. In Italy, whose government supports war, 85 percent of the public opposes it. Elsewhere, the figures are the same. In Thailand, for example, 75 percent oppose a war. In Uruguay, the figure is 79 percent. In Pakistan, it is 60 percent. Even in the United States, where poll results were mixed, a *New York Times* poll showed that 56 percent of the public favored war only with UN sanction. The news brought by these polls is political dynamite. Once upon a time, public opinion polls were of only secondary importance. Now, as every officeholder knows, they have moved to center stage. They are a prime currency of power: Poll numbers in the political realm are the equivalent of stock prices in the corporate realm. Polls are, in effect, periodic off-year elections, which not only may predict the real elections on which continuation in power depends but also affect the moment-to-moment ability of leaders to pass legislation, to rally the public to a cause and so forth. Their importance in the present context was revealed unmistakably when Gerhard Schröder of Germany and Roh Moo-hyun of South Korea won the leadership of their countries on peace platforms.

The worldwide demonstrations put faces on these numbers. It was as if the antiwar majorities around the world were saying, "You have heard about us in the opinion polls; you have seen our views expressed in percentages and graphs: how many are against war under any circumstance, how many against it without a UN vote, how many think it's all about oil and so forth. Well, here we are—in our millions, yet each of us a visible individual, carrying an individual sign, often homemade (in New York, one read, My Planet, Right or Wrong), as if some global schoolteacher had given us all the following assignment: Say what's wrong with the war on Iraq in ten words or less." The shift from answering a pollster's question at dinnertime to marching on the street was a critical one. Of all the possible forms of participation, giving your view to a pollster is probably the least active. Indeed, poll respondents *must* not be governed by self-propulsion, which is the essence of political participation; they must be chosen and contacted at random by the pollster. Otherwise, the result will be biased. Marching in a demonstration, by contrast, is among the most active forms of participation in political life. Demonstrators have bestirred themselves, put off other plans, braved the elements, flung themselves into action. They mean business. Even a passionate, engaged minority can, by appearing en masse in the streets, have a powerful influence on the body politic. When, as in the present case, the demonstrating minority is the tip of a majoritarian iceberg, the effect is multiplied many times over.

When terrorists attacked the Pentagon and knocked down the World Trade Center on September 11, everyone marveled that nineteen men had coordinated their actions for evil with such efficiency. On February 15, ten million coordinated their actions for good. February 15 was the people's answer to September 11.

The splendor of this global display of opinion was only thrown into sharper relief by the public silence in the countries where expression of public opinion is not allowed. The Chinese people were notably missing from the instant global agora. So were the North Koreans. The latter were in fact present at gigantic demonstrations—but these were compulsory ones, organized by the government, not to call for peace but to participate in grandiose and absurd birthday celebrations for the dictator Kim Jong Il. He loves his people so much that on his birthday he permits them to eat white rice two days in a row. In

Iraq, too, there were compelled demonstrations designed to mimic the spontaneous ones elsewhere, but there, as in North Korea, forced peals of praise for the head of state were the order of the day.

The leadership of the European Union, which had been divided on the war, got the point of the demonstrations on their continent soon enough. In a meeting of the EU's heads of state on Monday, it voted to give the UN inspectors in Iraq more time. It called for a peaceful solution—with war to be considered "only as a last resort"—because, the official statement said, "it is clear that this is what the people of Europe want." Romano Prodi, president of the European Commission, said even more simply, "People want peace." In fact, people wanted peace on every continent where public opinion could be measured.

One more element has been of the first importance. Not only has the human species made its will known; it also possesses an institution—now in session—for effectuating that will: the United Nations. The UN is often denigrated as a "debating society." One reason is that a "democratic deficit" is built into its very structure. No one elects its representatives. Like agency heads or cabinet ministers, they are appointees, creatures of government. To national publics, therefore, the UN often seems remote, abstract and, above all, powerless. The clear expression of the world's will repaired the UN's democratic deficit. It is entirely fitting at this moment that South Africa has invoked a provision of the Charter that permits the voices of countries of the General Assembly to be heard in the elite Security Council. The great majority have expressed opposition to war.

The UN delegates are still not elected, and the public is still not invited to sit at their councils, but now they have the wind of public opinion at their backs. They are "representatives" in a way that they have never been before. For the first time in the history of the institution, the "we the peoples of the United Nations" invoked in the UN Charter is not an abstraction. The "we" has spoken—not through its governments but directly to its representatives in the international body. Moreover, it has done so in the name of the goal that is the UN's prime reason for existing: peace. The United States and Great Britain have sought to use the UN as an instrument of war. The world has said No.

Can a war that the world and its assembled representatives have explicitly rejected still occur? Unfortunately, it can. Yet the events of February 15—and their repercussions in Europe and elsewhere—have radically altered the calculus of possibilities. Before the 15th, the war seemed unstoppable—inevitable. This alleged inevitability, indeed, has probably in fact been the strongest of the "arguments" for the war. Now, for the first time, it is conceivable that if enough people place enough specific, concrete pressure on their governments, the war can be prevented.

We—that is, we, the peoples of the earth—have examined the case for war against Iraq and rejected it. We have stepped forward onto the streets of our cities and looked at ourselves, and have liked what we saw. We know our will. Now we must act. We can stop the war.

American Tragedy

APRIL 7, 2003

THE DECISION TO go to war to overthrow the government of Iraq will bring unreckonable death and suffering to that country, the surrounding region and, possibly, the United States. It also marks a culmination in the rise within the United States of an immense concentration of unaccountable power that poses the greatest threat to the American constitutional system since the Watergate crisis. This transformation, in turn, threatens to push the world into a new era of rivalry, confrontation, and war. The location of the new power is of course the presidency (whose Augustan proportions make the "imperial" presidency of the Cold War look like a mere practice run). Its sinews are the awesome might of the American military machine, which, since Congress's serial surrender of the constitutional power to declare war, has passed wholly into the President's hands. Its main political instrument is the Republican Party. Its financial wherewithal is the corporate money that inundates the political realm. Its strategy at home is restriction of civil liberties, deep secrecy, a makeover in its image of the judiciary, subservience to corporate interests across the board, and transfer of personal wealth on a colossal scale from the average person to its wealthy supporters. Its popular support stems from fear engendered by the attacks of September 11—fear that has been manipulated to extend far beyond its proper objects. Its overriding goal, barely concealed behind the banner of the war on terrorism, is the accumulation of ever more power, whose supreme expression is its naked ambition to establish hegemony over the earth.

The steps in the rise of this power can be traced through international and domestic events. When the Soviet Union collapsed and the Cold War ended, the United States was left in a position of global privilege, prestige, and might that had no parallel in history. The moment seemed a golden one for the American form of government, liberal democracy. The American economic system was equally admired. In the previous two decades, a long list of nations—in southern Europe, in Latin America, in Asia—had chosen both systems, largely of their own free will. Even more astonishing, most of the peoples under the rule of the collapsed Soviet foe were making the same choice. The Soviet system had not only disintegrated; it had discredited itself. No rival was in sight. There were good reasons, even if one did not suppose that "the end of history" touted by Francis Fukuyama had arrived, for hoping that these trends would continue. A basically *consensual* rather than a *coerced* world seemed a real possibility.

Who could have guessed that barely a decade later the United States, forsaking the very legal, democratic traditions that were its most admired characteristics, would be going to war to impose its will by force upon an alarmed, angry, frightened world united against it? It's clear in retrospect that somewhere near the root of the problem was the very existence of the unchallengeable American military machine. In part, the imbalance with other nations was accidental. The machine had been built up in the name of containing the considerable military forces of the Soviet Union. When, against all expectation, the Soviet Union suddenly disappeared like a bad dream, the American giant found itself towering alone over the world. America likes to see itself as a force for good. Yet like all unchecked, unbalanced power, such might had, as the founders of this country knew so well, the potential to corrupt its possessors. The decade that followed was a mixed picture in which the raw arrogance of power was tempered by a lingering respect for the opinions of other nations and a search for common ground in the name of humanitarian objectives. In the first Gulf War, the will and the muscle to go to war were mainly American, but skillful diplomacy won the support or acquiescence of most nations, and the cause—repelling an act of aggression—won wide acceptance. In Kosovo, the United States acted without explicit United Nations agreement, angering many nations, yet the action was taken in the name of NATO, not merely the United States, and Serbian outrages on the ground helped create a climate of support around the world. The turning point, of course, came on September 11. Yet even then the United States gained considerable support for its first act of "regime change"—overthrowing the Taliban government of Afghanistan, which many understood as a measure of self-defense in the aftermath of a horrifying attack upon the United States. It was in the year that followed that the ambiguities of the 1990s were resolved in favor of the coherent, radical new policy of dominance asserted through the unilateral, preemptive use of force to overthrow other governments. The more clearly the Administration stated this policy, the more the world rebelled.

The path through domestic events to this same destination arguably begins with the impeachment attempt against President Bill Clinton, in which the Republican Party abused its majority power in Congress to try to knock a President of the other party out of the executive branch. The attempt failed, but the institutional siege on the presidency continued in the resolution of the freakishly close vote in Florida in 2000. In a further abuse of government power—in this case the judicial branch—the President was chosen by a vote not of the people of the United States but of the Supreme Court. The message of Republicans at the time in Congress and the Florida legislature was that if judges did not produce the result they demanded, they would bring on a constitutional crisis in the House of Representatives. A new conception of democracy was born: Freedom is your right to support what we want. Otherwise, you are "irrelevant." You can vote, but you do not decide. "Unilateralism" was born in Florida.

The tragedy of America in the post-Cold War era is that we have proved unequal to the responsibility that our own power placed upon us. Some of us became intoxicated with it, imagining that we could rule the world. Others of us—the Democratic Party, Congress, the judiciary, the news media—abdicated our obligation to challenge, to check and to oppose, letting the power-hungry have their way. The government of the United

States went into opposition against its own founding principles, leaving it to the rest of the world to take up our cause. The French have been better Americans than we have. Because the Constitution, though battered, is still intact, we may still have time and opportunity to recoup. But for now, we will have to pay the price of our weakness. The costs will be heavy, first of all for the people of Iraq but also for others, including ourselves. The international order on which the common welfare, including its ecological and economic welfare, depends has sustained severe damage. The fight for "freedom" abroad is crippling freedom at home. The war to stop proliferation of weapons of mass destruction in Iraq has provoked that very proliferation in North Korea and Iran. More ground has already been lost in the field of proliferation than can be gained even by the most delirious victory in Baghdad. Former friends of America have been turned into rivals or foes. The United States may be about to win Iraq. It has already lost the world.

The Other Superpower

APRIL 14, 2003

AS THE WAR began, Defense Secretary Donald Rumsfeld promised a "campaign unlike any other in history." What he did not plan or expect, however, was that the peoples of earth— what some are calling "the other superpower"—would launch an opposing campaign destined to be even less like any other in history. Indeed, Rumsfeld's campaign, a military attack, was in all its essential elements as old as history. The other campaign— the one opposing the war—meanwhile, was authentically novel. In the pages that follow, *The Nation* gives a snapshot of it in fourteen countries. If news has anything to do with what is new, then this campaign's birth and activity are the real news. What emerges is a portrait of a world in resistance.

Although there is an abyss of difference between the means of the two campaigns, there are also a few notable similarities. Both are creatures of the Information Age, which underlies the so-called "smart" technology on display in the war as well as the Internet, which has become the peace movement's principal organizing tool. Both are global—the United States seeks to demonstrate its self-avowed aim of global military supremacy, and the peace movement is equally determined to reject this. Not only is the whole world watching, as people used to say, the whole world is defending itself. Yet both campaigns are at the same time surprisingly agile, able to change their tactics and timing in response to events. Most interesting, perhaps, both conceive of power at least as much in terms of will as of force.

The first days of the war, for example, produced a surprise when the United States, instead of immediately showering missiles and bombs on Baghdad to produce "shock and awe," as predicted, instead carried out a limited strike aimed at killing Saddam Hussein and perhaps his sons. The goal, in the hideous phrase that now trips off so many tongues, was "decapitation" of the regime. Rumsfeld made clear the larger purpose in his briefing. He entertained the hope that the regime would collapse without a fight. "We continue to feel that there's no need for a broader conflict if the Iraqi leaders act to save themselves and to prevent such further conflict," he said, and proceeded to give these leaders a set of explicit instructions, as if he were already running Iraq: Do not destroy oil wells, do not blow up bridges, etc.

The unexpected twist in strategy generated a spate of admiring commentary. National Public Radio's Pentagon correspondent, Tom Gjelten, marveled that the new Administration policy was heavily "psychological." "The clear hope here was that somehow this regime will just collapse," he commented. "Maybe the war won't even be entirely necessary." And in an article called "A War of Subtle Strategy," the military analyst William Arkin called the new way of proceeding a "thinking man's war." In truth, however, the policy was less novel than the commentators were suggesting. History is filled with episodes of great armies drawing up before the gates of cities and demanding their surrender on pain of annihilation. (In Shakespeare's *Henry V*, for example, Henry menaces the inhabitants of Harfleur with plunder, rape and massacre if they do not yield up their town, and they do yield.) To have one's way without a fight is indeed the dream of every empire. Such is the strategy, for that matter, every time someone points a gun at someone else and orders "Hands up!" Far from being what Arkin calls a "middle ground—militarily and politically," such a tactic brings to perfection the policy of brute force—of shock and awe. The devastation threatened is so irresistible and crushing that its mere approach is meant to make the enemy surrender out of sheer terror. It aims to crush the will before the body is crushed.

Within a few days, however, the strategy of bloodless terror seemed to be foundering, as Iraqi forces proved willing to fight, and American and British forces were lured into cities where guerrilla operations against them began. A few early (and admittedly inadequate) indications suggest that the suffering people of Iraq, asked to choose between a dictator and a conqueror, wanted neither. In the words of one Iraqi opponent of the Hussein regime to the *New York Times* in the city of Nasiriya, "No Iraqi will support what the Americans are doing here. If they want to go to Baghdad, that's one thing, but now they have come into our cities, and all Iraqis will fight them."

The global peace movement, too, makes its appeal to the will, but in a diametrically opposite spirit. It encourages people not to give up their beliefs in obedience to the dictates of force but to act on those beliefs in the face of force. The war, we are told, is being fought for freedom. But who, we may ask, are the free ones—those who knuckle under to violence or those who defy it? The new superpower possesses immense power, but it is a different kind of power: not the will of one man wielding the 21,000-pound MOAB but the hearts and wills of the majority of the world's people. Its victories have been triumphs of civil courage, like the vote of the Turkish Parliament to turn down a multibillion-dollar bribe and, in keeping with public opinion, refuse the United States the use of Turkish bases in the war, or like the refusal of the six small, nonpermanent members of the United Nations Security Council to succumb to great-power browbeating and support its resolution for war. The question everywhere was which superpower to obey—the single nation claiming that title, or the will of the people of the earth. Outside the imperial counsels, the people of the earth were prevailing.

Never, in fact, had this will been expressed more clearly than in the moments leading up to the US assault. On the brink of the war no public but the Israeli one supported it under the conditions in which it was being launched—that is, without UN support. Public-opinion polls showed that in most countries opposition to the war was closer to unanimity than to a mere majority. A Gallup poll showed that in "neutral" (and normally pro-American) Switzerland the figure was 90 percent, in Argentina 87 percent, in Nigeria 86 percent, in Bosnia (recently the beneficiary of NATO intervention on its behalf) 91 percent. In all of the countries whose governments supported the war except Israel's, the public opposed it. The "coalition of the willing" was a coalition of governments alone.

A new phenomenon of rolling demonstrations circled the

world—not only in the great capitals but also in provincial cities and even small towns. (There was a demonstration in Afghanistan, the last scene of "regime change.") Most newspapers outside the United States opposed the war. UN Secretary General Kofi Annan expressed his chagrin. The Pope said the war "threatens the destiny of humanity." For once, the majority of the world's governments spoke up unequivocally for the majorities of their peoples.

The candles in windows did not stop the cruise missiles. The demonstrators did not block the tanks rolling north to Baghdad. Pope John Paul II did not stop President George W. Bush. Yet against all expectation, a global contest whose consequence far transcends the war in Iraq had arisen. Dr. Robert Muller of Costa Rica, a former assistant secretary general of the United Nations, caught the mood of the new peace movement when, at age eighty, he received an award for his service to the UN. He startled his discouraged audience by saying, "I'm so honored to be here. I'm so honored to be alive at such a miraculous time in history. I'm so moved by what's going on in our world today." For "never before in the history of the world has there been a global, visible, public, viable, open dialogue and conversation about the very legitimacy of war." This was what it looked like, he said, to be "waging peace." It was "a miracle." Shock and awe has found its riposte in courage and wonder.

The Limits of Interpretation

APRIL 21, 2003

A VESUVIUS OF violence has erupted from the dead center of American life, the executive branch of the government. No counterbalancing power, whether in the United States, the United Nations or elsewhere, has so far been able to contain it. Right now, it is raining destruction chiefly on one country, Iraq, half a world away from the United States. But others—Iran, Syria, North Korea—have already been named as candidates for attack. The war was launched in the name of a policy that asserts, in unusually explicit and clear language, an American claim of military dominance over all other nations on earth, which, in the words of George W. Bush, should bow to America's unchallengeable military might, give up any "destabilizing" attempt to catch up and restrict any further "rivalries to trade and other pursuits of peace." (The prospective world order that military rivalry to the United States would "destabilize" is, clearly, American global hegemony.) The pillars of this new policy of supremacy are too familiar by now to require much elaboration: American unilateralism, the replacement of the Cold War policy of containment with "preemption" and assertion of a right, at the pleasure of the United States, to overthrow other governments.

The war, indeed, is revolutionary in at least three distinct arenas. It is aimed, of course, at the destruction of the government in Iraq. It is aimed, further, at producing a political revolution in the entire Middle East. Finally, it announces the destruction of the existing world order (such as it is) in favor of one dominated by the United States. Just how radical this latter revolution is is suggested by some recent comments by one of the architects of the new policy, Richard Perle, until recently chairman of the Pentagon's Defense Policy Board. In a recent article in *The Guardian,* he wrote of the United Nations: "The chatterbox on the Hudson [*sic*] will continue to bleat." (How the UN can chatter and bleat at the same time is not explained.) But Perle's target is larger: "What will die is the fantasy of the UN as the foundation of a new world order. As we sift the debris, it will be important to preserve, the better to understand, the intellectual wreckage of the liberal conceit of safety through international law administered by international institutions."

In addition, a fourth revolution threatens—of the American constitutional order. In a culmination of the long decline of Congress's war power, the Congressional resolution authorizing this long-considered "war of choice" almost formally abdicated that choice and gave it to the executive. All that was missing was a surrender ceremony in which the defeated legislative branch handed over the war sword, placed in its hands more than two centuries ago by the country's founders, to the President.

Around the world, citizens and governments alike have read

and absorbed these announcements of America's global ambitions. With near-unanimity, they have reacted with alarm and dismay. Meanwhile, the war itself has aroused widespread revulsion. In the United States, however, where public opinion polls show that seven in ten people have rallied in support of the war, the picture is different. One of the peculiarities of the scene is the refusal of many of those supporters to acknowledge the larger policy in which it is embedded (if I may use that term). In early February, for example, the *Washington Post*, which has consistently favored the war, stated that it must not "be seen as an exercise in Mr. Bush's new doctrine of preemption, though ideologues on both sides would portray it as such." The formulation "ideologues on both sides" was arresting. One of those ideologues, after all, was evidently the President himself, who in the plainest terms has subscribed to the preemption policy and then named three nations—Iraq, Iran, and North Korea—that, as members of an "axis of evil," are targets. On the other "side" are citizens and commentators—I am one—who believe that the war is indeed the first application of the policy of preemption, not because we are ideologues but because the President and his Cabinet have repeatedly said that it is. The core of the policy is the Administration's resolve to stop the spread of weapons of mass destruction by military force. Preemption is necessary, the President has explained, because containment will not work. Perhaps the most important of the debates that are necessary, therefore, is whether this policy is workable or wise. That it is neither is strongly suggested by North Korea's acquisition—or decision to acquire—nuclear weapons and Iran's evident determination to do the same.

The attempt to save the war from its initiators and implemen-
tors has survived the war's beginning. Some of the war's supporters are upset to discover that the Administration's
explanations of its policies have been taken seriously by a horri-
fied world. They seem to be seeking some other way of looking
at the war that would be acceptable to the indignant international community. In England, for example, *Guardian* columnist
Hugo Young has counseled Prime Minister Tony Blair to save
himself from "taint" by distancing himself from certain particu-
lars of Bush's war policy. "What Iraqis see," he writes, "and the
world along with them, is a hegemon going about its business of
domination, and barely any longer interested in why it is hated
for doing so." He advises that Blair defy Bush and support UN
administration of a postwar Iraq. Here in the United States,
David Remnick of *The New Yorker* has taken a similar position.
There are, he admits, "conservative ideologues" in the Administration who "came to power with a grand, unilateralist project
and a palpable distaste for international institutions and
alliances"—but he calls them only a faction, as if the President
himself had not, in statement after statement, embraced their
agenda. He wants the war to be "rescued from the impulse to
make it part of a grander imperial project." Who will do it?
Remnick, too, emerges as a Blairite. Secretary of State Colin
Powell is also mentioned. But the war is not Blair's, nor is it
Powell's. It is Rumsfeld's war and Cheney's war and, above all,
it is Bush's war. The world believes this, and it is right. There is
no decent limited, multilateral war struggling to free itself from
the brutal, unilateral, hegemonic war. The war is what its
authors say it is. It cannot be interpreted into something else.

The Removed State

MAY 5, 2003

IN THE PAST 200 years, all of the earth's great territorial empires, whether dynastic or colonial, or both, have been destroyed. The list includes the Russian empire of the czars; the Austro-Hungarian Empire of the Habsburgs; the German empire of the Hohenzollerns, the Ottoman Empire, the Napoleonic Empire, the overseas empires of Holland, England, France, Belgium, Italy and Japan, Hitler's "thousand-year Reich" and the Soviet empire. They were brought down by a force that, to the indignation and astonishment of the imperialists, turned out to be irresistible: the resolve of peoples, no matter how few they were or how poor, to govern themselves.

With its takeover of Iraq, the United States is attempting to reverse this universal historical verdict. It is seeking to reinvent the imperial tradition and reintroduce imperial rule—and on a global scale—for the twenty-first century. Some elements, like the danger of weapons of mass destruction, are new. Yet any student of imperialism will be struck by the similarities between the old style of imperialism and the new: the gigantic disparity between the technical and military might of the conquerors and the conquered; the inextricable combination of rapacious commercial interest and geopolitical ambition and design; the distortion and erosion of domestic constitutions by the immense military establishments, overt and covert, required for foreign domination; the use of one colony as a stepping stone to seize others or pressure them into compliance with the imperial agenda; the appeal to jingoism on the home front. True, American officials state at every opportunity that they do not intend to "occupy" Iraq. But then the British in the nineteenth century said the same thing. Two years before the liberal Prime Minister William Gladstone ordered the conquest of Egypt he declared that his heart's desire was an "Egypt for the Egyptians." The liberal imperialist Lord Palmerston said in 1842 in defense of his gunboat diplomacy, "It is, that commerce may go freely forth, leading civilization with one hand, and peace with the other, to render mankind happier, wiser, better." When it came to rule, the British preferred, wherever possible, not "direct rule" but a sort of covert domination called "influence" or "indirect rule" or "paramountcy" (the British were as richly inventive of euphemisms as the United States is today). Then as now, imperialism, in the words of the great anti-imperialist Ernest Hobson, was "floated on a sea of vague, shifty, well-sounding phrases which are seldom tested by close contact with fact."

It was one thing, however, for Europeans, in newfound possession of modern tools of technical and organizational superiority, to subjugate "backward" foreign peoples in 1700 or 1800 or 1900. But can it be done again, in our century, in the wake of that project's universal rejection by the peoples of the earth? So far, the outlook is unpromising. The United States vowed to bring about "regime change" in Iraq. The phrase has rightly been criticized as an outrageously mild euphemism—a vague, well-sounding, shifty phrase if there ever was one—for an extremely violent act; but now it turns out that the expression defined a deeper problem. If I am going to change the oil in my car, I must, before I remove the old oil in the crankcase, have new oil ready to put in. Otherwise, my car will quickly overheat and break down on the road. This is roughly the condition of Iraq two weeks after the destruction of its former government. The United States, it turns out, forgot to bring a new government with it when it set out from Kuwait to Baghdad. The troops brought plenty of MREs (meals ready to eat) but no GRR (government ready to rule). American forces had no intention of becoming a police force, Brig. Gen. Vincent Brooks told the press. Did the Administration perhaps take its own slippery rhetoric about not occupying Iraq too seriously? The result was a vacuum of authority soon filled by nearly universal looting. Many Iraqis made clear their hatred of the old regime and their joy at its disappearance; but it appears that they had little more confidence in the invader. Finding themselves caught between local misrule and foreign rule, did they perhaps decide that they had a momentary opportunity to grab something for themselves and set about sacking their own country? A journalist, upon arriving in an Iraqi city, described it as "prelooted." Did the Iraqis, in anticipation of foreign exploitation, "preloot" their whole country?

The United States thus achieved Regime Removal but not the promised Regime Change. There were, we can now see, no plans even to keep order in Iraq, much less to administer it, or organize a government there. The famous war plan was much discussed; the peace plan, it appears, did not even exist.

This became clear when Defense Secretary Donald Rumsfeld referred to the raging anarchy in Iraq as "untidy," and America's new viceroy in Iraq, retired Gen. Jay Garner, newly arrived in the city of Nasiriyah from the Hilton hotel in Kuwait, likened events to the American constitutional convention of 1787, remarking rhetorically, "I don't think they had a love-in when they had Philadelphia." Does he really think that mayhem in Iraq, including the extinction of the better part of the country's cultural treasures, has any resemblance to the deliberations by which Washington, Franklin, and Madison framed the Constitution of the United States? Is such a man fit to run a country?

So far, the American military giant has proved to be a political pygmy. The Shiite cleric Abdel Majid al-Khoei, who was imported into Iraq from London by the "coalition" forces, was promptly hacked to death by local people. The gathering of Iraqis invited by the United States to meet at a US military base has been boycotted by the country's most important political groups. In Mosul, American troops have fired upon an angry mob, killing seven. "It's a show of force, but people don't understand it," a soldier in Mosul told the *Times*. "They're not grateful."

Before the war began, it was often said that winning the war would be easy and winning the peace hard. And it was surely always clear even to the war's opponents that the United States could drive its tanks from Kuwait to Baghdad, whereupon the regime of Saddam Hussein would dissolve. Yet was it ever certain that what followed the conventional engagements would be a peace? With every day that passes, "the peace" looks more like another war.

The Governors of Baghdad

IN BAGHDAD THIS week, one Mohammed Mohsen Zubaidi, an Iraqi businessman with ties to the Iraqi National Congress, has shown up claiming to be the city's governor. He's set up in the Palestine Hotel, where he meets with local leaders, offers to solve their problems and announces plans to get the city's services back on their feet. However, the head of the INC, Ahmad Chalabi, has declined to support Zubaidi's pretensions, and in a recent confrontation between the two and their armed guards, there was accidental gunfire. Chalabi makes no claim to be governor, but he, too, has shown up in Baghdad and started meeting with local leaders, in preparation for an interim government that the United States wants to set up. The United States itself has appeared in the person of Gen. Jay Garner, the intended temporary administrator of all Iraq. He, too, has brought a governor of Baghdad with him: one Barbara Bodine, former Ambassador to Yemen. Just now, it's hard to say which of them, if any, will actually wind up running Baghdad.

Among these pretenders to power, the Garner team has one

notable qualification: It represents the occupying power that has just overthrown the former government. The problem has been that the United States has so far declined to act in the classic manner of the conqueror: It has offered no substitute government. Rather, it has come in the guise of a liberator. The normal thing for a conqueror to do once it has routed the indigenous forces is to declare martial law and start giving orders. That is what the United States did on the two occasions most often cited as precedents for the Iraq war—the conquest and occupation of Japan and Germany after the Second World War. The United States made no claim that it was "liberating" those peoples. It conquered them and dictated the forms of their political future, which they, happily, came to accept and approve over time.

The nature of a conqueror's rule has always been well understood. The citizens of the subject population obey because otherwise they can be put to death, just as the soldiers of their defeated army were. The seventeenth-century political philosopher and archrealist Thomas Hobbes had a name for this kind of obedience. Putting to himself the question, "Despotical dominion, how attained?" he answered that it depended on the "consent of the vanquished." He cited the Roman example— highly pertinent in these days of American imperial ambition. The Romans achieved conquest "not by the victory but by the consent of the vanquished." He explained that "it is not . . . the victory that giveth the right of dominion over the vanquished but his own covenant. Nor is he obliged because he is conquered, that is to say, beaten, and taken, or put to flight; but because he cometh in, and submitteth to the victor." The act that symbolized this consent was the surrender—as in the ceremony on the battleship Missouri when General Umezu signed a surrender agreement with General MacArthur.

This second transaction, the one that turns military victory into conquest, is the one that has not occurred in Iraq. The United States has not demanded—and the Iraqis have not given—any kind of consent. They cometh not in; they submitteth not. Except in the Kurdish north, where Garner was recently received joyously, Iraqis have been telling reporters that while they indeed hated the regime of Saddam Hussein they also do not want to be governed by the United States. Almost with one voice, they say, "No to Saddam, No to Occupation." Or, more disturbingly, "No to America, No to Secular State, Yes to Islamic State."

On the surface, there might appear to be a coincidence of interest here: The Iraqis don't want the United States in Iraq and the United States doesn't want to be there. The rub, of course, is that the United States is not in fact ready to let the Iraqis themselves determine their own future and has published thirteen principles that must guide the formation of Iraq's new government. They include democracy, federalism, respect for women, and rejection of "political violence." In the immediate future, the physical reconstruction of the smashed, looted country is a necessity. Many observers judge that these tasks will require many years and the expenditure of many tens of billions of dollars.

Yankee, go home! Yankee, stay! Which will it be? Defense Secretary Rumsfeld's formulation is that the United States will stay as long as is necessary "and not a day longer." But how long is that to be? Six months? Two years? Five years? Twenty?

The question involves much more than timing. It involves fundamental decisions, so far evidently unmade, about the role of the United States not only in Iraq but in the entire Middle East, for which the United States has planned an ambitious political makeover. Questions of governance, indeed, extend far beyond that region. Most permanent members of the Security Council have made clear their conviction that the international interlocutor for any future Iraqi government, interim or permanent, should not be the United States at all, but the United Nations. Nor are the decisions of the Security Council "irrelevant" in the current situation. Although the UN has no troops on the ground in Iraq, it has formal control over Iraq's oil revenues, now under embargo except for the purchase of permitted items, such as food. The embargo will end one way or another— but into whose hands will Iraq's oil revenue be placed? General Garner's? Ahmad Chalabi's? Mohammed Mohsen Zubaidi's?

For events are moving fast. As the outside pretenders to power were jockeying in Baghdad, Iraqis, many of them Shiite Muslims who neither had any connection with the United States nor wanted any, were setting about actually governing large swaths of Iraq, including parts of Baghdad. They were erecting roadblocks, stopping looting, restoring services. For them, as one put it, cooperation with the United States is "accursed"— the mark of the quisling. What if these groups simply go about the business of organizing their country independently of Garner, or in defiance of him? And what if, further, they choose not the sole superpower but the United Nations as their link with the world? In that case, Garner and the country he represents will face a decision: whether to withdraw or try to do what conquerors in the past have always done: impose their will on the conquered people by force.

Backing Up

MAY 19, 2003

NOW THAT THE regime of Saddam Hussein has been overthrown, the Bush Administration, like a submarine that, having successfully sunk one ship, resurfaces its periscope to find others, is looking about the world to see what countries it may decide to attack. Since these prospective wars, like the one against Iraq, would be "wars of choice," it's hard for dizzied citizens to guess which nations, if any, are next. Syria? The Administration leveled charges like those it made against Iraq: possession of weapons of mass destruction, support for terrorism. Of such stuff is "regime change" made. "There's gotta be change in Syria as well," Deputy Secretary of Defense Paul Wolfowitz told *Meet the Press*. But then the President said he had no plans to attack Syria just at this minute. He stated, "I have no specific operation in mind at this point in time. I can't think of a specific moment or incident that would require military action as we speak." It was a reprieve—for the time being. Perhaps Iran? An Administration spokesman lamented Iran's "intervention" in Iraq's domestic affairs. (This from a country that has just overthrown the government of Iraq and now occupies the country.) But the nation most often mentioned is North Korea, which has announced that it actually possesses nuclear weapons—the sort of weaponry of mass destruction that the toppled Saddam regime was accused of building but which so far has turned out not to have had after all. At the antiwar demonstrations this past winter, participants sometimes chanted, "This is what democracy looks like." The military occupation of Iraq and all the talk about who might be next is what empire looks like.

The dilemma posed by the North Korea crisis is distressingly clear-cut. On the one hand, North Korea has announced that it has nuclear weapons and intends to keep them and make more unless the United States forswears any attack upon it and makes other concessions. (The United States has independently confirmed that North Korea does indeed have one or two nuclear weapons. Curiously, however, the facts remain in doubt. Both governments have a reason to practice deception on this point: the North Koreans in order to increase deterrence, the Bush Administration in order to push the failure to stop proliferation back into the Clinton years.) On the other hand, George W. Bush has declared that "the United States of America will not permit the world's most dangerous regimes to threaten us with the world's most destructive weapons"—and then named North Korea (along with Iraq and Iran) as one of the countries in question. If both regimes remain on their present course, there must be a collision. And if there is a collision, one of two things must happen: Either North Korea must throw up its hands and disarm or the United States, in a second application of its preventive policy, must wage another war. Defense Secretary Rumsfeld has already circulated a memo calling for "regime change" in North Korea. But war against North Korea will be a different matter from war against Iraq. North Korea possesses 700 fighter jets, 3,700 tanks, about 700 missiles capable of hitting South Korea and Japan and 11,000 artillery pieces within range of South Korea's capital and largest city, Seoul. Even if nuclear weapons are not used, there may, military analysts have stated, be as many as one million casualties on the *first day* of the war. The war will of course go on for more than one day. And if nuclear weapons are used—by North Korea, the United States, or both—this figure must be multiplied many times over. In sum, hard as it is to concentrate on a new war in Asia, we must start waking up to the fact that the crisis over North Korea is incomparably more dangerous than anything that has happened or is likely to happen in Iraq.

There is, however, a perfectly obvious solution to the crisis. It would be a deal in which each side accepts the main demand of the other: North Korea would give up its nuclear program and the United States would give the requested security guarantee and economic help. The United States fears harm from North Korea's nuclear weapons, but North Korea builds those weapons because it fears attack by the United States. The two countries have no quarrel but the quarrel itself. No other tangible bone of contention—no territorial dispute, for example—divides them. The solution is to declare the quarrel over, and act accordingly. Indeed, on October 12, 2000, in the last days of the Clinton Administration, the United States and North Korea did exactly that. They declared, "Neither government would have hostile intent toward the other." Or, as North Korea expert Leon Sigal has characterized this statement, "In plain English, we are not enemies."

Certainly, no one can say that the choice between war and acceptance of a nuclearized North Korea will have been forced upon the United States until such a settlement has at least been proposed. What is far from obvious, unfortunately, is that either government is ready to accept a deal fashioned along these lines. Until very recently, the position of the United States was that it would not even enter into talks with North Korea until North Korea first agreed to roll back its nuclear program. Now talks have begun, but the United States has not yet indicated a readiness to give the requested guarantees. The President has called the North Korean position "blackmail." North Korea, for its part, may or may not be willing to give up its nuclear weapons program even in the event that it receives the guarantees it demands. It may be using the current talks with the United States as a ploy to buy time while it produces nuclear weapons. Then, with a larger nuclear arsenal in hand, it would bargain from a position of strength. Such a position is one the United States would be in an excellent position to understand. The US government has always believed that negotiations must be conducted from a position of strength. Unfortunately, history offers no example of a country that itself built and then surrendered its nuclear arsenal in the face of external threats.

As in the Cuban missile crisis forty-one years ago, diplomacy is given the task of escaping traps created by rigid, belligerent, unwise military threats and commitments. The arts we need now are the ones not of winning but of backing up.

A Nuclear Education

MAY 26, 2003

IN THIS SPACE last week, I commented that the choice for the United States in North Korea was probably between a catastrophic war and permitting North Korea to keep its nuclear program and its reported small nuclear arsenal, and I suggested that of the two alternatives the second, though itself highly undesirable, was the better. It was anything but obvious, however, that such a course would be adopted, much less that this would happen just one week later. Yet the retreat may in fact now be under way. According to the *New York Times*, the Bush Administration has given up its goal of preventing North Korea from acquiring nuclear weapons and instead will concentrate on stopping it from exporting nuclear materials to others. "The President said that the central worry is not what they've got, but where it goes," an Administration official told the paper. But since, as the *Times* points out in an accompanying editorial, this goal is as unlikely to be achieved as preventing the creation of the materials in the first place, it's hard to escape the conclusion that the new policy is anything more than a fig leaf designed to disguise the failure of the old policy. In effect, the Administration has decided that in the case of North Korea, at least, proliferation is better than war.

The reversal of policy is dramatic. Let us recall that in his State of the Union address in 2002, delivered four months after the attack of September 11, the President declared what in effect was an ultimatum to proliferators: "The United States of America will not permit the world's most dangerous regimes to threaten us with the world's most destructive weapons." He placed three regimes in the "worst" category—Iraq, Iran, and North Korea—and famously called them an axis of evil. His policy up-ended the precedents of half a century. Previously, the United States had pursued nonproliferation solely by diplomatic and political means. It had never attacked a nation to stop it from obtaining either nuclear weapons or any other weapon of mass destruction. Now the Bush Administration proposed to stop proliferation by force.

The United States has just forcibly removed the regime in Iraq in pursuit of the President's policy. The proclaimed goals of the war were two: to seize weapons of mass destruction allegedly possessed by that regime and to demonstrate to other countries what might happen to them if they seek weapons of mass destruction. Quite recently, the President stated that "any outlaw regime that has ties to terrorist groups, and seeks and possesses weapons of mass destruction, is a grave danger to the civilized world, and will be confronted." In the meantime, however, the North Korean regime has been learning an opposite lesson. It decided that the path to safety—the way to avoid "regime change" by the United States—was not to forgo nuclear weapons but to obtain them immediately in order to have, in its words, a "powerful deterrent." In making this decision, the North Korean government was not doing anything unusual. From the first days of the nuclear age down to the present, nuclear proliferation has been driven by the fear of nuclear attack by others. Even the United States, the world's first nuclear proliferator, built the bomb because it feared that Hitler would get one first. Later, the policy of preventing nuclear attack by threatening nuclear retaliation was formalized in the strategy of nuclear deterrence, which became an almost unchallengeable dogma during the Cold War years.

But after September 11, Bush declared that deterrence was inadequate to our new post-Cold War realities and that he stood ready to launch "preemptive" (actually preventive) war, as he has just done in Iraq. It has turned out, however, that the deterrence policies that were being dropped by the United States were at the same time being taken up by North Korea. Now the United States itself has been deterred by nuclear arms, and it is preventive war that has had to be dropped. The bomb, once the hallmark of a "superpower," has become an equalizer in the hands of small, poor nations.

The remaining "axis" country, Iran, seems to be seeking the same solution to its vulnerability in the face of the American threat. Although it forswears any intention of building nuclear arms, it has, like North Korea, announced that it possesses a uranium-enrichment program. It seems very unlikely that the United States will be able to practice violent "regime change" against Iran. The United States will have its hands more than full in the years to come trying to impose its will on the Iraqi people, who as yet show little sign of accepting American rule. Any attempt to attack and occupy Iran would be a further step into this quagmire.

In short, the Bush policy of stopping proliferation of weapons of mass destruction by force has failed. In Iraq, no weapons of mass destruction have been found, and with every day that passes it seems unlikely that any weapons significant enough to justify the war will be discovered. In North Korea, a vigorous nuclear program not only exists but evidently has proved unstoppable by military means. In Iran, a nuclear program is in full swing, and the prospects of preventing it by force seem nil. Not even full democratization of that country, should the people of Iran choose this path, will insure denuclearization. All factions in Iran are agreed that their country has the right to counter Israel's nuclear arsenal by building one of its own.

As welcome as is the Administration's apparent choice of proliferation over war, it leaves the United States without a nonproliferation policy. One must be found. Otherwise the emergence of North Korea, and probably of Iran, as nuclear powers will lead to still another round of proliferation in North Asia and the Middle East. The failure of the Bush policy offers some lessons. One is that nuclear possessors make bad enforcers of nonproliferation. Every possessor was in fact once a proliferator, and possession by one country has always in fact been the motor of proliferation by others. The process is not stopped but speeded up by a policy of forcible disarmament—"counterproliferation"—which places the United States in the hopeless position of defending a global double standard by force. Nuclear disarmament, like virtue, must begin at home.

Madmen

JUNE 2, 2003

DURING THE COLD WAR, nuclear strategic doctrine was riven by a fundamental contradiction. Governments thought it sensible to threaten nuclear war—the better to "deter" a foe from doing something unwanted—yet it obviously made no sense actually to wage nuclear war, for this led to the famous "mutual assured destruction." But if carrying out the threats was senseless, then how could it be frightening? What use were they? Wouldn't the foe, supposing that no country would be demented enough to "assure" its own destruction, disbelieve the threats and do what it pleased in spite of them?

The high strategists of nuclear defense scratched their heads and came up with answers. One was to take technical and other steps that deliberately put your nation on what the strategist Thomas Schelling called a "slippery slope." That is, if you visibly arranged to make yourself a little bit out of control, the foe would no longer be able to imagine that you might desist from nuclear war in a last-minute fit of sanity. They'd think that you might plunge into the abyss in spite of yourself. And so they would fear you, as hoped. (The inexorable mobilization schedules of World War I acted thus, once diplomacy had broken down, to assure the start of a war that was in no one's interest.) Another solution, also pioneered by Schelling, among others, was the deliberate cultivation of a reputation of irrationality. Schelling called this policy the "rationality of irrationality." In this policy, the foe would believe in your self-destructive threats not because it thought you might slip on a banana peel, so to speak, at the brink but because it believed you just might be lunatic enough to go over the edge deliberately.

Richard Nixon was one practitioner of this strategy. When he came to office, he planned to end the Vietnam War on terms favorable to the United States by frightening North Vietnam and the Soviet Union into compliance. He hoped, by persuading them that he was just a little bit off his rocker, to scare them into submission. He called the strategy the "madman theory." In practice, however, it failed. The Russians and the North Vietnamese ignored the threat and went on to win the war.

When the Cold War ended, most people probably bid an unfond farewell to these blood-freezing paradoxes, along with the Soviet-American nuclear arms race that had given rise to them. They may be surprised, therefore, to find them returning in the new context of what many call the second nuclear age (the first having consisted of the Cold War). Recently, the United States— the world's "only superpower," or "hyperpower," as the French say—has found itself in a nuclear stalemate with tiny, poverty-stricken but (probably) nuclear-armed North Korea. North Korea has rediscovered the madman theory with a vengeance. It cannot be in the interest of North Korea, to state what is sickeningly obvious, to get into a nuclear war with the United States. At the moment, North Korea is incapable of striking American soil with a nuclear-armed missile. At the most, it can fire a few nuclear weapons at South Korea or Japan. The United States, of course, has more than 10,000 fully deliverable nuclear bombs. And yet North Korea's Dear Leader, Kim Jong Il, has been bellowing nuclear destruction at the United States. His country possesses, his spokesmen have said, a "powerful deterrent" that can turn South Korea—and the American bases in South Korea—into a "sea of fire" (a phrase the North Koreans seem almost to have copyrighted). Just recently, North Korea declared its promise to South Korea not to build nuclear arms "nullified"—owing to America's threats to destroy the regime.

Kim is well suited to the role of madman. This leader (with his accidentally fashionable spiky, two-inch-tall hair) of a regime that has starved millions of its people and is perhaps the most regimented on earth, does not have to strain to convince the world that he might be capable of irrational acts. And yet it's also true that those acts display—shades of Thomas Schelling— the "rationality of irrationality" more clearly than anyone has done before, since the United States has indeed been deterred (at least so far) by his threats.

Yet there is no need to go halfway around the world to find the resurrection of the madman theory. We only have to look at our own government. The Bush Administration has been puzzling again over the paradox that a threat is no good if it appears crazy to carry it out. Linton Brooks, the acting administrator for the National Nuclear Security Administration, has said to *The New York Times*, "We need to make sure our weapons will in fact be seen by other countries as a deterrent. One element of that is usability. If nobody believes there is any circumstance where you will use the weapon, it is not a deterrent." Therefore the Administration has proposed that a legislative ban established in 1993 against low-yield nuclear weapons (less than five kilotons of explosive power) be rescinded, and the Senate Armed Services Committee, voting largely on party lines, has just concurred. The change is in keeping with a broader revival of nuclear threats by the Administration, which also revived the production of the plutonium pits that are at the core of nuclear bombs, which wants to shorten the time necessary to resume testing and which seeks funds to study a new nuclear weapon called the Robust Nuclear Earth Penetrator. (It's hard to know when this Administration is merely tone-deaf to the overtones of its jargon and when it is deliberately trying to provoke its opposition with outrageous nomenclature.)

However, the trouble, once again, is that if you establish usability, you may get use. And is the first use of nuclear weapons since Nagasaki what the United States now seeks? And can the United States succeed in persuading other nations not to acquire nuclear weapons when it insists not only on possessing them but on using them, and what is more, using them first? Carl Levin, the ranking Democrat on the Senate Armed Services Committee, comments, "This just undermines our whole argument. We're driving recklessly down a road that we're telling other people not to walk down." And what if, as you cultivate your own new version of the madman theory, your adversary does the same, as Kim Jong Il now is doing? One madman leaves the hope that the adversary may be sane. Two could push us all into the sea of fire.

Thinking Movement, Working Demonstration

JUNE 23, 2003

IN THE MONTHS before the American-Anglo invasion of Iraq, the peace movement was out on the streets demonstrating. Since the fall of the Iraqi regime, it has been less in evidence. But the silence does not mean inactivity. The movement is thinking. What are its responsibilities toward occupied Iraq and its people? What are the occupation's implications for the Middle East? For the world? What should the United Nations do now? What should the target of protest be? What are the connections between war abroad and the attack on civil liberties and social justice at home? What vision of a better world can the movement offer? And then there is the inescapable corresponding question: What should be done? How big should the movement's tent be? Should the global justice and the global peace movements merge? What should the role of the environmental movement be? To what extent should the US movement join the global movement and to what extent preserve a separate identity? What is its role in the 2004 election?

These questions and others are being asked at hundreds of meetings and in an infinity of conversations, memos and e-mails. For example, on April 26 US Labor Against the War passed a resolution stating, "American working families face a domestic crisis. This crisis has been intensified by the Bush administration's foreign and domestic policies of military intervention abroad and neglect at home that benefit corporations and the wealthy at the expense of working families." In Jakarta in May, representatives of major peace and justice groups around the world met and endorsed a document called the "Jakarta Peace Consensus." The Green Party is broadening its agenda to include issues of peace and justice. At the University of California, Irvine, the Citizen Peacebuilding Program held a meeting of West Coast peace groups to take stock and plan for the future. In Washington, several conferences have jostled for attention: one held by Tikkun Community, an offshoot of *Tikkun* magazine, and one called Take Back America, organized by the Campaign for America's Future. The broadest of the US umbrella groups, United for Peace and Justice, is convening a meeting in Chicago to make its plans.

Anybody with ten minutes of experience in politics will recognize that a process of reflection and planning of this breadth is similar to what must occur when people are founding a political party—that is, a collection of people prepared not just to protest an existing order but to change it and to take responsibility for the results. For a peace and justice party, the concentration on "economics" would be replaced by a concentration on *justice* (the economy must serve society, rather than the other way around), and the concentration on "security" would be replaced by a concentration on *peace* (that is, security would be sought through peace, not war). Yet such words as "movement" and "party" are themselves under reexamination. A richer understanding of activism and the way it can change the world is developing. "History," Rebecca Solnit comments in her essay "Acts of Hope" in *Orion* magazine, "is shaped by the groundswells and common dreams that single acts and moments only represent." And the same may be true of movements and parties.

But, of course, there is no Peace and Justice Party, not globally and not locally, nor is there likely to be one anytime soon, and so the question of what to do concretely in the near future remains in the foreground. One date that fairly leaps off the calendar is August 30, 2004, when the Republican Party will begin its convention in New York City, just a few miles from the World Trade Center crater. The time and place were chosen by the GOP for their rich symbolism. The peace and justice movement is likely to show up en masse to do the same. A confrontation of epic proportions may be in the making. Medea Benjamin, a founding director of the global justice organization Global Exchange, foresees "a day of action against the empire." She proposes the message, "The World Says No to Bush." Some activists, she reports, are considering a "huge global electronic vote" for or against the United States imperial ambitions. She also wants the global justice movement to "come to Middle America." The question of whether the global justice movement and the global peace movement would merge, she says, was in fact answered by the worldwide antiwar demonstrations of February 15, when the two became one on the ground. The merged stream will come to New York in August 2004.

Other activists are concentrating more on the elections of 2004. David Cortright, president of the Fourth Freedom Forum and a member of the guiding committee of the antiwar organization Win Without War, proposes concentrated efforts to defeat Bush in swing states. "Everybody's attention is focused on regime change at home," he comments. "How to do that is less clear. On the one hand, it's easy to understand that we have to be in these battleground states, such as Florida, Ohio and Michigan—not so much in California and New York. But the peace movement also has to address the question of security and the threat of terrorism. Bush can't run on the economy and the environment, but he can run on the fear of the threat of terrorism. Bush political adviser Karl Rove has indicated that's what they intend to do." The potential for conflicts between the local and the global strategies is obvious. A substantial portion of the electorate may resent what they would see as "foreign" intervention in American electoral affairs. Asked if she feared a nationalist backlash in the United States, Medea Benjamin answered, "I almost welcome it." The world is affected by American decisions, she explains, and has a right to participate in them. Cortright approves of demonstrations at the Republican convention but wants them to be "handled right." He says, "The message has to be that the people of New York say no to Bush's attempt to exploit their city for political advantage." He also believes, for reasons both principled and tactical, that any and all demonstrations should be rigorously nonviolent. On the one hand, a movement against violence must not itself be violent. On the other hand, a nonviolent movement is less likely to anger voters.

The relationship of the movement to the election presents

other questions. In the United States, the movement now represents a minority view. The need, as at other times in recent US history (including the anti-Vietnam War and civil rights movements), is to bring this minority view into the mainstream. Yet to achieve anything, the movement must first exist. To that end, places for it to exist must be created. It seems unlikely—unless and until another war is launched—that serial mass demonstrations will continue. Demonstrations are well suited to sharply defined objectives, not to broad goals. On the other hand, the needs of the time are too urgent for just the usual fare of speeches, conferences and so forth.

A global protest at the time of the Republican convention has an inescapable logic that is already propelling events but leaves other needs unmet. First, it is more than a year away. What to do in the meantime? In that meantime, the Democratic Party—the only vehicle with a realistic chance of producing a candidate who can defeat Bush—will have chosen its standard-bearer. Second, the New York demonstration blurs the specifically American responsibility for choosing its own government, which will, after all, be selected by American voters on November 2 of that year. Third, the New York demonstration will in its nature emphasize what it is against more than what it is for: Its time and place, after all, will have been chosen not by itself but by Rove.

Additional venues would appear to be in order. One is needed, I suggest, that is a mass event but not only a protest. Call it a working demonstration. Models have been offered on the global scale by the World Social Forum, which last met in Pôrto Alegre, Brazil, and next will meet in Mumbai, India. At a working demonstration, tens of thousands would assemble not to stand facing a single platform listening to speeches (some of which are interesting and some of which are not) or to march in protest but to attend a profusion of speeches and seminars; to scoop up literature from hundreds of booths; to confer in countless formal and informal meetings—to educate one another, to network, to agitate, to plan, to extend, to discover and strengthen common purposes. In such a meeting, the activity of the movement is not merely represented but conducted.

The aims of the event—to promote peace, justice and democracy and oppose the imperial path—would deliberately be defined loosely. It would be diverse and boisterous. It would be highly televisable. It would not be the instrument of any political party, but it would announce to the world the existence of a new political force. It would be a place for free speech, unpopular speech, provocative speech, unbuttoned speech. Timing is important. A choice of this November would still leave time to organize it and would position it to pour energy into the election campaigns about to begin. If a working demonstration is the place for a movement to be fully itself, then elections are the place for compromises—even, it may be, for the choice of lesser evils.

In short, the movement must learn to walk and chew gum at the same time. Just because the movement had established places where it could show itself and be itself without reserve, its members would feel free to work for whatever portion of their agenda they judge is really achievable in the elections of 2004. Such intervention in mainstream politics is a sine qua non of a serious movement. But success in the mainstream will not come without first building independent strength. Courage, like fear, is contagious, and those who are afraid to be themselves can never persuade others of the justice of their cause.

No Doubt

JUNE 30, 2003

IT IS NOTORIOUSLY difficult to prove a negative. At what point can you be sure that something does not in fact exist? For example, if I lose my glasses and begin to search for them in my apartment, when do I abandon the search and conclude: I must have left them at the office? Is it when I have checked all the pockets in my wardrobe? Looked under all the cushions in the apartment?

So it goes with the search for weapons of mass destruction in Iraq. Certainty may not come for a long time. Let's add that it was entirely reasonable to argue—though some disagreed— that Saddam Hussein possessed such weapons. After all, it's a matter of record that he had them before the Gulf War, and the United Nations inspectors sent in after the war to destroy them reported that some materials were still unaccounted for.

But questions of fact cannot be resolved by thinking. Evidence is required. And if the evidence is used to justify a war, then it must be both unchallengeable and readily producible. Before the war, the Bush Administration stated on dozens of occasions and in the most unequivocal terms that it had such evidence. Now—nine weeks after the end of Saddam's regime—it is clear that no evidence of the required quality existed. The public trust was abused. The world was deceived. That the unequivocal evidence was missing before the war will remain a fact even if, somewhere down the road, weapons of mass destruction are found. "We know where they are," Defense Secretary Donald Rumsfeld said. But he did not know. How could he, when the intelligence agency of his own Defense Department was stating that there was "no reliable information on whether Iraq is producing and stockpiling chemical weapons, or where Iraq has—or will—establish its chemical warfare agent production facilities." The war was fought on false premises. One might hope that some of the war's supporters would now reconsider their position. I know of no such case. Instead, we have been presented with an entire bestiary of excuses—ones so inventive, it has some interest in its own right.

1. *The UN Said So.* Columnist Robert Kagan of the *Washington Post* has written an almost touchingly plaintive column listing all those who credited the mistake, as if widespread belief could make falsehood true. Among those mentioned are not only President Clinton and other Clinton officials but, of all people, the leaders of Germany and France—temporarily de-demonized for the purpose. Even the head of the UN inspection team, Hans Blix, is cited. In fact, of course, Blix never stated, as the Bush Administration did, that there were weapons of mass destruction but only that there was *some evidence that there might be* weapons of mass destruction. The crux of the argument was whether the inspectors should be

given more time to resolve doubt into certainty—one way or another. The Administration itself has joined in the unexpected rehabilitation of the UN. The White House communications director, Dan Bartlett, has said there is proof of an Iraqi weapons of mass destruction program because "the UN Security Council passed a resolution that confirmed it."

2. *The War Was Really About Something Else.* There are innumerable variations on this theme. Senator John McCain, who once toured the country in a bus called The Straight Talk Express, now says, "The American people support what the President did, whether we find those weapons or not, and they did so the day they saw nine- and ten-year-old boys coming out of a prison in Baghdad." It seems that the straight talk McCain required of candidates is not needed by Presidents. None other than arch-hawk Deputy Defense Secretary Paul Wolfowitz has said the choice of the WMD justification had "a lot to do with the US government bureaucracy, we settled on the one issue that everyone could agree on, which was weapons of mass destruction as the core reason."

The idea that the war was really about something else all along has been especially popular among its more liberal supporters. Former *Nation* columnist Christopher Hitchens reserves "the right" to be for the war for reasons other than those given by the Administration. Thomas Friedman, who, it must be said, never did express worry about Iraqi weapons of mass destruction and instead supported the war as a way to "democratize" the Middle East, confesses, "I have to admit that I've always been fighting my own war in Iraq." The trouble, of course, is that Hitchens and Friedman are not deciding policy. The world doesn't get the war as described in their columns; it gets the real war the Administration actually is fighting. They are supporting a phantasm.

3. *They Didn't Really Mean It.* In an editorial dismissing the importance of the evidentiary fiasco, the *Washington Post* admits, "Some of the claims tossed off by Vice President Cheney and other senior officials in the heat of the debate appear unlikely to be borne out." Very likely the Vice President of the United States just got carried away when, in a prepared speech on August 26 to the Veterans of Foreign Wars, he announced, "Simply stated, there is no doubt that Saddam Hussein has weapons of mass destruction." And perhaps the President was merely hot under the collar when he used the "no doubt" language in his last press conference before the launch of the war.

4. *We've Already "Found the Weapons of Mass Destruction."* This from the President himself, in a statement made in Poland, referring to trailers found in Iraq that may or may not have been built to produce biological weapons. But soon he seemed to take it back, stating at the military base in Doha, Qatar, "We're on the look" for the weapons. A few days after that, he shifted again: "I am absolutely convinced with time we'll find out they did have a weapons program." As things stood at that moment according to the President, his Administration had (1) found weapons of mass destruction but (2) not yet found a weapons of mass destruction program. The facts on

the ground showed nearly the opposite: inconclusive evidence of a program (the trailers) but no weapons. So "programs" and "weapons" were now the same and our government had at the same time found and not found both. The President seemed bent on demonstrating, publicly and swiftly, the factual illiteracy that his Administration demonstrated secretly and in slow motion as it took the United States to war.

Cognitive Torture

JULY 14, 2003

A SMALL JOURNALISTIC cottage industry has grown up demonstrating that the Bush Administration took the nation to war against Iraq under false pretenses. The industry has been highly productive. Administration officials claimed certain knowledge that Iraq possessed weapons of mass destruction when they had no such knowledge. They claimed that the Iraqi government was seeking uranium ore from Niger months after the CIA had already disproven the charge. They claimed that Iraq had ties with Al Qaeda in the absence of any evidence of such ties, and much evidence to the contrary. When the intelligence agencies produced conclusions the Administration didn't like, it pressured them to come up with different conclusions. And so forth.

A parallel but less noticed collapse of Administration policy has been occurring with regard to another region. As early as the State of the Union address, George W. Bush announced a radical change in US policies for dealing with the proliferation of weapons of mass destruction. The United States, the President said, would "prevent" the spread of the weapons by the pre-emptive use of military force. "We will not permit the world's most dangerous regimes and terrorists to threaten us with the world's most destructive weapons." The words "will not permit" are the words of an ultimatum. They place the military prestige of the country making them on the line as clearly as language can. The threat was of course carried out in Iraq—with the nugatory results just mentioned.

In another country, North Korea, however, the nuclear programs were real. They were not only real; they led (according to both the North Korean and the US governments) to the actual production of nuclear weapons. Yet the United States did nothing. Administration spokesmen repeatedly declared that North Korea's acquisition of nuclear arms was "not a crisis." How, observers demanded to know at the time, could it be a crisis for Iraq to have a nuclear weapons program (which then was still thought to exist) but not a crisis for North Korea to have an actual nuclear arsenal?

Since then, the United States has backed off even further, declaring that the new American objective is merely to prevent North Korea from exporting its nuclear materials. The United States would "absolutely not" permit such behavior, Secretary of State Powell told Tim Russert on *Meet the Press.* An Administration official told *The New York Times,* "The President said that the central worry is not what they've got but where it goes." But the fact remains that the clearly articulated threats of the world's only superpower in regard to the most serious issue facing it and the world—nuclear danger—turned out to be hollow. Yet the debacle has been met with silence.

Those who rejected the original strategy as reckless and unworkable didn't call Bush to account, because they liked the default better than the policy. Those—most of them Republicans—who approved of the policy stayed silent because they didn't want to criticize a President of their own party. One group likes the collapse on substantive grounds; the other won't attack it on political grounds. (Yet even now, Republicans excoriate President Clinton for accepting the negotiation of an Agreed Framework with North Korea to deal with its nuclear program in 1994.) In truth, as Michael Levi of the Brookings Institution has pointed out in *The New Republic*, stopping exports is as infeasible as preempting North Korea's nuclear program was in the first place. The new goal is merely a way of saving face.

In one respect, the treatment of Iraq and North Korea were opposite: In the first, the United States knocked out a government to get at nuclear weapons that, as far as we know, weren't there; in the second it backed off in the face of nuclear weapons (and a large conventional force) that were there. But in another respect, the policies were alike: The words and commitments made by the Administration on one day had evaporated the next.

The sequel in Iraq was also surprising. A month after American forces had taken control of Iraq, they had not secured its nuclear facilities. Had the Administration, knowing full well that it was deceiving the public about Iraqi weapons of mass destruction, failed to take its own claims seriously because it knew they were not true?

A further wrinkle in this increasingly strange story came recently when the President said (in words already cited in this space) that the United States has "found weapons of mass destruction." He was referring to two vans discovered in Iraq that may or may not have been built to produce biological weapons. If someone states to the world that he has a black dog when he does not, he is lying. But what do you call it if, in full sight of all, he says he has a black dog while pointing to a white dog?

It is cognitive torture. Just as hypocrisy is the tribute that vice pays to virtue, a lie is the tribute that vice pays to truth: The element of concealment pays respect to the hearer's demand to be told what is true. But if the "lie" is out in the open—if any fool can see that the dog is white—then truth itself is disrespected.

At that moment, attention must shift from the deceiver to the deceived. The corruption threatens to spread from the teller to the hearer—from the Administration to the country, from them to us. Today lies, exaggerations, contradictions and broken promises litter the mental landscape, like uncollected garbage, polluting and poisoning the intellectual and moral air. A fog of amnesia covers the scene. What was said ten minutes ago is forgotten. What was promised yesterday never appears, and no one cares. What is needed now is not so much more investigation as an awakening of will. The question is no longer what the government is doing but whether the public will hold it to account. Does the public like to hear the lies as much as the Administration likes to tell them, or will our self-respect demand a response? Cognitive torture calls for cognitive indignation. And indignation should lead to action.

Imposing Our Will

AUGUST 4, 2003

THE UNITED STATES seems to interpret the news these days
through a prism of catchphrases borrowed from history. Once,
the phrases of the Second World War—"Munich," "appease-
ment" and so forth—were applied to the Vietnam War, with
calamitous results. Now, the catchphrases of the Vietnam War
are being pressed into service to describe the war on Iraq:
"search and destroy," "quagmire," "winning hearts and minds,"
"the Baghdad triangle." Because I began my life as a journalist
in the latter's namesake—the "iron triangle," a center of resistance near Saigon—I'm perhaps more likely than most to see any
American war as "another Vietnam"; but for the same reason I
recognize a need to hold the Vietnam-Iraq comparison up to
scrutiny. The differences between the two conflicts are large and
obvious. In Vietnam, America's enemy had powerful rear-guard
support—in the first place, uninvaded North Vietnam; in the
second place, the People's Republic of China and the Soviet
Union, an acknowledged superpower. Today, the Iraqi resistance has no proven state support, and the United States is the

world's "sole superpower." (The rear-area support that is likely
to appear over time is international Islamic terrorism—a very
significant force but hardly equal to China or the Soviet Union.)
In Vietnam, the resistance forces had a half-century of contin-
uous experience fighting colonial occupiers—first the French
then the Japanese, then the French again and only last the Americans. Iraq, on the other hand, was an independent country when
attacked by the United States. In Vietnam, national consciousness has roots that extend back hundreds of years. Iraq was cobbled together by the British in 1920. The Vietnamese resistance
was Communist, but the Iraqi resistance is of unknown political
complexion and seems to combine many elements. The Vietnam
War was fought to stop the spread of Communism; the war on
Iraq was allegedly fought to stop the spread of weapons of mass
destruction.

But the similarities are equally obvious, and becoming more
so every day. As in Vietnam, conventional American forces in
Iraq face guerrilla resistance. As in Vietnam, an end to the Iraq
war—a successful "exit strategy," to use the post-Vietnam
catchphrase—depends on setting up a regime that can stand on
its own and be acceptable to the United States. As in Vietnam,
military forces have thus been given an essentially political task.
As in Vietnam, political events will be more important than military ones. The politics in question are American and Iraqi. In
America, the question is how long the public will endure a steady
stream of casualties and expenditures. (Already, polls are
showing a sharp drop in public support for the war.) In Iraq, the
fundamental question is whether the Iraqi people will accept or
reject a US-founded regime. The outcome of the war will

depend above all on the wills of the two peoples and their inter-action. The more Iraqis hate and resist the occupation, the more Americans are likely to grow tired and force an end to the war, as they did in Vietnam.

The outlook for success is doubtful, and the reasons go deep into history. They are ones that we Americans, of all people, should well understand. We have recently celebrated the Fourth of July, the day we announced our claim "to assume among the Powers of the Earth the separate and equal Station to which the laws of Nature and of Nature's God entitle them." Arguably, the modern principle of national self-determination was born at that moment. Since then, almost every nation in the world has pursued the same path, with the result that the great empires of the nineteenth and twentieth centuries, from the British to the Soviet, have been dispatched to history's ash heap. The passion for independence from colonial rule, which Leonard Woolf called "the world revolt," has proved universal and, what is more surprising, has been all but universally successful. Is Iraq destined to be an exception—a country that, having achieved its independence, now gives it up again to a foreign power?

Not all the differences between Vietnam and Iraq, moreover, are favorable to the United States. For one thing, the stated goal of the war—finding weapons of mass destruction—has melted away. The short war to save America from nuclear destruction has turned into a long war with no clear purpose. For another thing, whereas in Vietnam the United States intervened in sup-port of an existing government, in Iraq it intervened to over-throw a government. True, the government in South Vietnam depended wholly on American money and military power for its survival and had almost no independent source of strength in its own society. Still, it did have the signal, underappreciated virtue of existing: It employed thousands of people, delivered the mail, picked up the garbage. In Iraq there is no such creature. It's not for nothing that conquerors set up quisling regimes. The Administration that promised "regime change" delivered only regime smash. In a colossal omission, it forgot that Iraq would after all have to have some sort of government or other.

This is something new. The American combat forces, who had been told that the road home goes "through Baghdad" were hastily enlisted to fill the political deficit. They found themselves trying to repair electrical lines, govern towns, guard banks. But immediately Iraqis, who quickly proved not to be missing the self-determination gene, turned against them, and some began to attack them. A new American administrator, L. Paul Bremer, was brought in to impose a new, tough policy. In his words, "We dominate the scene and we will continue to impose our will on this country." When this strategy, so drastically at odds with any idea of democracy or self-determination, appeared to backfire, Bremer reversed course and decided to appoint the "Governing Council" of Iraq that has just come into existence. Now he seeks to perform a miracle even more remarkable than any that was required in Vietnam—to create out of thin air a regime that will do America's will without the presence of American forces. Today, people are asking how long the United States "will have to stay" until success is achieved, but this masks the more important question of whether the mission is possible at all. The real question may be how long the United States can bear to stay before failure is accepted. In Vietnam, it took more than a decade.

Ways to Win

EVENTS HAVE SUDDENLY and unexpectedly handed the Democratic Party an opportunity to defeat George W. Bush in 2004. His main justifications for his war in Iraq (existence of weapons of mass destruction, connections with Al Qaeda) have collapsed, while the war itself intensifies. At home, his tax cuts have sent deficits out of control and jobs are disappearing at a gallop. Each of these conditions seems likely to be either chronic or permanent: The prospect of finding actual weapons of mass destruction, though conceivable, has dimmed to the vanishing point; the cost in blood and treasure of the occupation seems likely to increase; the deficit is likely to remain high or get higher. On other issues—health care, the environment, education—the public trusts Democrats more than it does the President. His poll numbers have fallen, from the high sixties and mid-seventies a month or two ago to the mid-fifties today.

But it's one thing for Bush to fail, another for the Democrats to succeed. Debate within the party is sharpening. The questions for the antiwar wing of the party are especially acute. In a winner-take-all electoral system like ours, anyone who holds views that are outside the mainstream is faced with an obvious and inescapable dilemma: Should one vote for a candidate one agrees with wholeheartedly but seems likely to lose the election or vote for a candidate one doesn't much care for but seems likely to win? Which is worse, a noble defeat or an empty victory?

I can give myself as an example. I opposed the war in Iraq before it was launched and now regard it as a mounting disaster, with the worst yet to come. But according to a recent NBC News/ *Wall Street Journal* poll, 69 percent of the public still think the war was worth it. Obviously, I'm out of step with the public. The candidate who best reflects my views is Dennis Kucinich. He not only opposed—and still opposes—the war; he wants to cut the Pentagon budget and shift the direction of American foreign policy toward peace and cooperation with the rest of the world. Second best from my standpoint is Howard Dean, who also opposed the war but now wants the United States to stay the course and keep Pentagon spending at present levels. Dean, as everyone knows, has been gaining support and appears to have a real chance to win the nomination. So, for me, Kucinich would be the more principled choice, Dean the more pragmatic choice. Yet Dean's views on the war, too, are outside mainstream opinion and could doom him in the general election. The cautionary example usually given is George McGovern, who rightly opposed the war in Vietnam in 1972 but lost to Richard Nixon in a landslide. Ever since, the Democratic Party has been running away from "McGovernism."

Other candidates propose to dive deliberately and immediately into the mainstream. One is Joseph Lieberman. In his words, the party must "go right up the middle." He says anyone who (like Dean) "was opposed to the war against Saddam, who has called for the repeal of all of the Bush tax cuts . . . could lead the Democratic Party into the political wilderness." Lieberman himself probably believes that the war was right, and that full repeal of the tax cuts would be wrong, but in this appeal he is clearly asking those of us who disagree with him to forget our beliefs and support him on purely pragmatic grounds. "The middle," of course, is, of mathematical necessity, the place that any candidate must be in if he is to win. And it's easier to move to the mainstream than to move the mainstream to you. (On the other hand, selling your principles for power doesn't always work. Quite often there are no buyers for the tarnished goods. President Clinton was admittedly a master of the art; but Lieberman doesn't seem to have the knack. You do not get to the middle by trumpeting "I am in the middle." You do it by saying things people in the middle like to hear. Claims to be in the middle are inside baseball, not the game itself. When candidates step up to the plate, they should swing at the pitch, not give commentaries on their batting technique.)

As it happens, McGovern, not merely a historical figure but a living person, and a thoughtful and articulate one at that, has jumped into the discussion. Calling the warnings against McGovernism "political baloney," he comments that although in 1972 he won only Massachusetts and the District of Columbia, "no war could have continued long after that election." He is suggesting that although the movement against the Vietnam War, of which his campaign was a powerful expression, never put a President in office, it nevertheless forced an end to the war.

His point is that political influence can be exerted in more than one way: "Give me a presidential candidate who speaks the truth as he sees it, and I'll show you a candidate whose campaign, win or lose, will be good for the nation."

Other episodes in American history teach a similar lesson. When Lyndon Johnson signed the Civil Rights Act of 1964, he had the support of both Houses of Congress, including a majority of Republicans. But the politically acute President saw that the triumph had an immense future electoral cost attached. "I think we just gave the South to the Republicans," he commented. And indeed, in years to come the GOP, following the "Southern strategy" adopted by the same Richard Nixon who defeated McGovern, won the South from the Democrats, laying the basis for successes in the next several elections. And so even as civil rights was winning substantively, it lost politically. The public accepted the message but rejected the messengers, as it would also do with McGovern. Yet the victory was real: The nation was changed for the better. The national holiday born of the movement is Martin Luther King Day, not Richard Milhous Nixon Day. There will never be a Richard Milhous Nixon Day. Neither will there probably be a George McGovern Day, but posterity will honor him.

These episodes do not necessarily teach Democrats whom to vote for in 2004, but they do suggest some lessons. Victory does not come through the ballot box alone. It sometimes comes by circuitous paths. Electoral politics should be played to win, yet changing hearts and minds can at times be as important as changing the President. McGovern is right. When in doubt, it's best to err on the side of speaking the truth.

The Importance of Losing

September 22, 2003

THE BASIC MISTAKE of American policy in Iraq is not that
the Pentagon—believing the fairy tales told it by Iraqi exile
groups and overriding State Department advice—forgot, when
planning "regime change," to bring along a spare government to
replace the one it was smashing; not that, once embarked on running the place, the Administration did not send enough troops to
do the job; not that a civilian contingent to aid the soldiers was
lacking; not that the Baghdad museum, the Jordanian Embassy,
the United Nations and Imam Ali mosque, among other places,
were left unguarded; not that no adequate police force, whether
American or Iraqi, was provided to keep order generally; not
that the United States, seeking to make good that lack, then
began to recruit men from the most hated and brutal of
Saddam's agencies, the Mukhabarat; not that, in an unaccountable and unparalleled lapse in America's once sure-fire technical
know-how, Iraq's electrical, water, and fuel systems remain dys-
functional; not that the Administration has erected a powerless
shadow government composed in large measure of the same

clueless exiles that misled the Administration in the first place; not that the Administration has decided to privatize substantial portions of the Iraqi economy before the will of the Iraqi people in this matter is known; not that the occupation forces have launched search-and-destroy operations that estrange and embitter a population that increasingly despises the United States; not that, throughout, a bullying diplomacy has driven away America's traditional allies.

All these blunders and omissions are indeed mistakes of American policy, and grievous ones, but they are secondary mistakes. *The main mistake of American policy in Iraq was waging the war at all.* That is not a conclusion that anyone should have to labor to arrive at. Something like the whole world, including most of its governments and tens of millions of demonstrators, plus the UN Security Council, Representative Dennis Kucinich, Governor Howard Dean and this magazine, made the point most vocally *before* the fact. They variously pointed out that the Iraqi regime gave no support to Al Qaeda, predicted that the United States would be unable to establish democracy in Iraq by force—and that therefore no such democracy could serve as a splendid model for the rest of the Middle East—warned that "regime change" for purposes of disarmament was likely to encourage other countries to build weapons of mass destruction, and argued that the allegations that Iraq already had weapons of mass destruction and was ready to use them at any moment (within forty-five minutes after the order was delivered, it was said) were unproven. All these justifications for the war are now on history's ash heap, never to be retrieved—adding a few largish piles to the mountains of ideological claptrap (of the left, the right and what have you) that were the habitual accompaniment of the assorted horrors of the twentieth century.

Recognition of this mistake—one that may prove as great as the decision to embark on the Vietnam War—is essential if the best (or at any rate the least disastrous) path out of the mess is to be charted. Otherwise, the mistake may be compounded, and such indeed is the direction in which a substantial new body of opinion now pushes the United States. In this company are Democrats in Congress who credulously accepted the Bush Administration's arguments for the war or simply caved in to Administration pressure, hawkish liberal commentators in the same position, and a growing minority of right-wing critics.

They now recommend increasing American troop strength in Iraq. Some supported the war and still do. "We must win," says Democratic Senator Joseph Biden, who went on *Good Morning America* to recommend dispatching more troops. His colleague Republican John McCain agrees. The right-wing *Weekly Standard* is of like mind. Others were doubtful about the war at the beginning but think the United States must "win" now that the war has been launched. The *New York Times,* which opposed an invasion without UN Security Council support, has declared in an editorial that "establishing a free and peaceful Iraq as a linchpin for progress throughout the Middle East is a goal worth struggling for, even at great costs." And, voicing a view often now heard, it adds, "We are there now, and it is essential to stay the course." Joe Klein, of *Time,* states, "Retreat is not an option."

"Winning," evidently, now consists not in finding the weapons of mass destruction that once were the designated reason for fighting the war but in creating a democratic government in

Iraq—the one that will serve as a model for the entire Middle East. Condoleezza Rice has called that task the "moral mission of our time." Stanford professor Michael McFaul has even proposed a new Cabinet department whose job would be "the creation of new states." The Pentagon's job will be restricted to "regime destruction"; the job of the new outfit, pursuing a "grand strategy on democratic regime change," will be, Houdini-like, to pull new regimes out of its hat. On the other hand, the Center for Strategic and International Studies, which recently produced a report on the situation in Iraq, thinks a big part of the problem is bad public relations and counsels "an intense communications and marketing campaign to help facilitate a profound change in the Iraqi national frame of mind."

These plans to mass-produce democracies and transform the mentalities of whole peoples have the look of desperate attempts—as grandiose as they are unhinged from reality—to overlook the obvious: First, that people, not excluding Iraqis, do not like to be conquered and occupied by foreign powers and are ready and able to resist; and, second, that disarmament, which is indeed an essential goal for the new century, can only, except in the rarest of circumstances, be achieved not through war but through the common voluntary will of nations. It is not the character of the occupation, it is occupation itself that the Iraqis are, in a multitude of ways, rejecting.

The practical problem of Iraq's future remains. The Iraqi state has been forcibly removed. That state was a horrible one; yet a nation needs a state. The children must go to school; the trains must run; the museums must open; murderers must be put in jail. But the United States, precisely because it is a single foreign state, which like all states has a highly self-interested agenda of its own, is incapable of providing Iraq with a government that serves its own people. The United States therefore must, to begin with, surrender control of the operation to an international force. It will not suffice to provide "UN cover" for an American operation, as the Administration now seems to propose. The United States should announce a staged withdrawal of its forces in favor of and in conjunction with whatever international forces can be cobbled together. It should also (but surely will not) provide that force with about a hundred billion or so dollars to do its work—a low estimate of what is needed to rebuild Iraq.

Biden says we must win the war. This is precisely wrong. The United States must learn to lose this war—a harder task, in many ways, than winning, for it requires admitting mistakes and relinquishing attractive fantasies. This is the true moral mission of our time (well, of the next few years, anyway). The cost of leaving will certainly be high, just not anywhere near as high as trying to "stay the course," which can only magnify and postpone the disaster.

And yet—regrettable to say—even if this difficult step is taken, no one should imagine that democracy will be achieved by this means. The great likelihood is something else—something worse: perhaps a recrudescence of dictatorship or civil war, or both. An interim period—probably very brief—of international trusteeship is the best solution, yet it is unlikely to be a good solution. It is merely better than any other recourse. The good options have probably passed us by. They may never have existed. If the people of Iraq are given back their country, there isn't the slightest guarantee that they will use the privilege to create a liberal democracy. The creation of democracy is an organic process that must proceed from the will of the local people. Sometimes that will is present, more often it is not. Vietnam provides an example. Vietnam today enjoys the self-determination it battled to achieve for so long; but it has not become a democracy.

On the other hand, just because Iraq's future remains to be decided by its talented people, it would also be wrong to categorically rule out the possibility that they will escape tyranny and create democratic government for themselves. The United States and other countries might even find ways of offering modest assistance in the project. It's just that it is beyond the power of the United States to create democracy for them.

The matter is not in our hands. It never was.

Politics in Command

29 SEPTEMBER 2003

AMERICAN POLICY IN Iraq is reaching a moment of crisis. American troops are stretched thin, and the US is considering calling up more reserves. The American team sent to find weapons of mass destruction in Iraq reportedly have found none. The Bush administration's request for $87 billion for the war has, according to polls, met with public rejection. Bush's approval ratings have declined. But most important are events in Iraq itself. It's commonplace to say that the United States, having won the war in Iraq, is now in danger of losing the peace. This view, however, is forgetful of the most famous saying of the theorist of war Carl von Clausewitz—that war is the continuation of politics by other means. Military victory, he is saying, is not sought for its own sake, but to achieve a political goal. If that goal is lost, the war is lost. In other words, to lose the peace is to lose the war.

The Vietnam War, which I observed as a reporter, offers an illustration. The United States defeated the enemy in almost every battle in Vietnam. For more than a decade, the United

States won and won and won, monotonously—until it lost. The reason was that its military victories were untranslatable into political victories. And without political victory—without the creation of a regime in South Vietnam that was satisfactory both to its own people and to the United States—the moment of withdrawal had to be the moment of defeat. Since the American public was not prepared to let its government fight in Vietnam forever, the defeat was foreordained, and protraction of the conflict brought only unnecessary bloodshed.

True, Iraq is not Vietnam. In Vietnam, the communist opposition had been resisting foreign occupation for the better part of a century, was in charge of half the country, and enjoyed the backing of two major powers, China and the Soviet Union. The Iraqi resistance enjoys no such advantages. (However, it does enjoy support from the global extremist Islamic movement.) But a fundamental similarity is still present: in order to be able to withdraw from Iraq without defeat, the United States must somehow oversee the creation of a government in Iraq that satisfies both the Iraqi people and itself. Regime change (a revolutionary policy) requires regime-creation—a requirement that our offshore Robespierres in Washington seemed until recently to have overlooked. Absent this, the choice will be the same as the one in Vietnam: indefinite occupation or withdrawal and defeat.

That is why one needs to pay closer attention to political developments than to the latest rocket attacks on American forces or car-bombings. Guerrilla war is not always successful. Only if the guerrillas enjoy the political support of the population can they become a decisive force. Otherwise, their own society rallies against them, and they are defeated or reduced to a chronic nuisance. On the other hand, an aroused popular will can be hugely effective without any guerrilla arm at all, as the Solidarity movement in Poland—to give just one example—demonstrated.

So far, almost no spontaneous, active political support for the American occupation of Iraq appears to have developed. A story by Anthony Shadid in the *Washington Post* illustrates the apparent trend of events. In the town of Khaldiya, an officer who was part of a force just trained, equipped, and financed by the US told Shadid, "In my heart, deep inside, we are with them against the occupation. This is my country, and I encourage them." When the people you recruit support your enemies, you are in deep political trouble. You may in fact be training the force that is attacking you. The political development of the US-appointed governing council tells the same story. Its most prominent members, including the Pentagon's favorite, Achmed Chelabi, are demanding that the occupation authorities quickly hand over sovereignty to the council. The council seems to appreciate that its future in Iraq will be dim if it doesn't align itself with the public's dislike of the continued occupation.

The sentiment of the officer in Khaldiya is of a kind that proved almost universal in the twentieth century—the longing of peoples to expel foreign invaders and run their own countries. In Iraq, it contends in many Iraqi hearts and minds with gratitude to the United States for destroying the brutal regime of Saddam Hussein, but if other news reports are correct, the resentment is swiftly gaining the upper hand. In politics, gratitude is generally a short-lived phenomenon. For example, when the Ayatollah Mohammad Bakr al-Hakim, a leader of Iraq's

Shiite majority, which was savagely suppressed by the Hussein regime, was murdered along with more than a hundred others in a bombing in Najaf, his brother, Abdel-Aziz Hakim, a member of the governing council, declared, "The occupation force is primarily responsible for the pure blood that was spilled."

In sharp contrast, a recent Gallup poll taken in Baghdad showed that 67 percent of the people thought their lives would be better five years hence than they were under Hussein. Curiously, the same poll found that President Jacques Chirac of France enjoyed a 42 percent favorable rating, while President Bush stood only at 29 percent. Whatever the validity of these confusing findings, which run contrary to most other firsthand accounts by reporters, they serve as a reminder to pundits or others that the will of a people that has lived under dictatorship for decades is not a simple thing to read.

But doesn't the US, in any case, want exactly what the Iraqi people want—independence and freedom for Iraq? And hasn't the United States already embarked on a program of Iraqization? The word, of course, recalls Nixon's policy of Vietnamization, and, like that policy, conceals a difficulty. The United States doesn't want just any Iraqization; it wants Iraqization that suits American interests. Would the United States, for example, accept an Iran-style Shiite-dominated Islamic republic in Iraq? "That's not going to happen," Secretary of Defense Rumsfeld has already said. What about partition of the country—as happened peacefully in Czechoslovakia and bloodily in Yugoslavia? What if the Iraqi people, eyeing Iran's nuclear program and Israel's nuclear arsenal, democratically decide to build nuclear weapons or other weapons of mass destruction? It's one thing to want

Iraqis to take control of their own country, but quite another to accept the Iraq that they create for themselves. Even if democratic procedures are successfully implanted in Iraq, the choices that the Iraqi people make may be dramatically at odds with any or all of the purposes that sent the US into Iraq in the first place.

Already, the signs of growing political divergence from American wishes are clear. In these circumstances, it may be that the longer the occupation lasts, the less influence the US will have. In one respect, however, the administration seems to be correct. One way or another, the Iraqi people really will decide their own future. Whether the result is one the administration cares for is another question altogether.

Learning the Obvious

OCTOBER 6, 2003

SOMETIMES WHEN I feel I want to raise my voice against the American folly in Iraq, my zeal is infected with boredom. I get the urge to say that the war in Iraq is worsening the nuclear proliferation problem (Iran and North Korea are speeding up their nuclear programs in part in order to avoid regime change); that there is no proven alliance between Saddam Hussein and Al Qaeda; that we are inflaming the peoples of the Middle East against us; that we are driving away even our traditional European allies by our highhanded policies; that we are making ourselves less secure, not more. But then I realize that these things are by now obvious, and to state what is obvious is boring. I want to say them not because they are fresh and interesting but because they are not heeded. But if to state the obvious is boring, then to repeat it is the very definition of boredom. The point was impressed on me when I read a quotation in the indispensable website Tomdispatch (www.tomdispatch.com) from President George H.W. Bush's memoir, *A World Transformed*, which was written with Brent Scowcroft. Bush was talking about why he did not overthrow Saddam Hussein at the end of the first Gulf War:

> Trying to eliminate Saddam . . . would have incurred incalculable human and political costs. Apprehending him was probably impossible. . . . We would have been forced to occupy Baghdad and, in effect, rule Iraq. . . . there was no viable "exit strategy" we could see, violating another of our principles. Furthermore, we had been self-consciously trying to set a pattern for handling aggression in the post–Cold War world. Going in and occupying Iraq, thus unilaterally exceeding the United Nations' mandate, would have destroyed the precedent of international response to aggression that we hoped to establish. Had we gone the invasion route, the United States could conceivably still be an occupying power in a bitterly hostile land.

I couldn't have said it better myself. And this was written five years ago, by the father of the current President. So much for feeling brilliant for insisting upon such things now.

I'm reminded of my experience as one of those who opposed the war in Vietnam. In the mid-to-late 1960s, we tirelessly pointed out that the war was mainly a nationalist rebellion against foreign occupation, not mainly an advance probe of world Communism; that the issue could only be solved politically, not militarily; that the war was weakening, not strengthening, the United States; that the only solution was to withdraw America troops—and so on and so forth. We considered ourselves brave for saying such things, all of which were rejected by mainstream opinion. And yet at that time, too, the antiwar arguments were obvious, or soon became so. Just how obvious is revealed by Kai Bird's excellent biography of William and McGeorge Bundy, *The Color of Truth*. Bird reveals that as assistant secretary of state, William Bundy—widely seen as a Vietnam hawk—confessed in a 1964 paper that "a bad colonial heritage of long standing, totally inadequate preparation for self-government by the colonial power, a colonialist war fought in half-baked fashion and lost, a nationalist movement taken over by Communism ruling in the other half of an ethnically and historically united country, the Communist side inheriting much the better military force and far more than its share of the talent—these are the facts that dog us today." Bird says that in this sentence Bundy prefigured "just about all the points that I.F. Stone, Bernard Fall or other early critics of the war would make within a year."

Even more striking is a conversation in 1964 between President Lyndon Johnson and Richard Russell, chairman of the Senate Armed Services committee. "I don't believe the American people ever want me to [abandon Vietnam]," Johnson told Russell. "If I lose it, I think they'll say I've lost it. . . . At the same time, I don't want to commit us to a war," Russell's answer was a prophecy that turned out to be exact. A full-scale effort would "take a half million men," he said. "They'd be bogged down in there ten years." In short, all the arguments against the war were privately well-known—obvious—to the Administration. Yet it plunged deeper and deeper into the war.

Why? There appear to be two closely related answers. One is political. As Johnson's comment hints, ever since the United States had "lost" China to Communism in 1949, it was considered politically fatal to "lose" another country. As McGeorge Bundy wrote to Johnson, "The political damage to Truman and

Acheson from the fall of China arose because most Americans came to believe that we could and should have done more than we did to prevent it. This is exactly what would happen now if we should seem to be the first to quit in Saigon." The second answer was strategic. Policy-makers of the day believed that nothing in the foreign policy of the United States was more important than American "credibility." If American power was defeated anywhere, they believed, it might crumble everywhere. The idea of a strategic retreat was ruled out. Both motives, then, had to do with power—in the first place, domestic political power, in the second, global power.

Today, too, the obvious is trumped by the argument of power. The need therefore is not just to produce more facts and better arguments (though those are always needed) but to challenge the powers that uphold illusion. The best antidote is the counterforce of public opinion, which means, in the last analysis, the force of voting. Today, as in Vietnam thirty years ago, it is possible to win this battle. In the Vietnam years, public opinion gradually changed. It drove a President—Lyndon Johnson—out of office. It forced another, Richard Nixon, to end the war, and then he was driven out of office, too. Today, public opinion is already shifting. A recent ABC-*Washington Post* poll records that 60 percent of the public opposes George W. Bush's request to Congress for $87 billion for the war. The antiwar candidate Howard Dean has become the acknowledged front-runner for the Democratic nomination. In some polls, Bush's overall approval ratings are in negative territory. This is the kind of argument that Presidents understand.

The question is, How many more people, American and Iraqi, will have to lose their lives to teach our leaders the obvious?

Accountability

OCTOBER 27, 2003

". . . interviews last week with historians, advertising executives, pollsters and Democratic and Republican image-makers turned up this consensus: Mr. Bush has to do a better job—or at least a more extensive job—of selling Americans on Iraq and the American occupation, no matter what anyone might think of the policy itself."

—ELIZABETH BUMILLER, *The New York Times,*
"Hard Sell: In a Democracy, the President Is Also Salesman in Chief"

"Everything that happened yesterday is irrelevant."

—Advice for Bush from G. CLOTAIRE RAPAILLE,
a French-born medical anthropologist who has done psychological
consumer research for Seagram, Procter & Gamble, and Ford,
quoted in the same article

A YEAR HAS passed since Congress authorized George W. Bush to launch a war against the regime of Saddam Hussein in Iraq. Each of the justifications for the war put forward by the Administration has now proved either entirely imaginary or so remote as to appear fanciful. The President said that the United States must go to war because Iraq possessed weapons of mass destruction and was ready to use them, but the American team, led by David Kay, sent to discover those weapons has now, after four months of searching, had to report that it has found none.

The President said that Saddam gave support to Al Qaeda, but no such support has been demonstrated. The President said he was going to war to establish a democracy in Iraq so splendid that all the Middle East would emulate it (Iraq would be "a dramatic and inspiring example of freedom for other nations in the region," he said in February), but six months after the war's end Iraq remains virtually without a government, and resistance to the American occupation is on the rise. The United States has been led into war on false pretexts before. A case in point is the provoked and falsified attacks on American naval vessels in the Tonkin Gulf, which were used to stampede Congress into voting for the Tonkin resolution authorizing the Vietnam War. But never before has an Administration's entire justification for war—not just its triggering incident—proved to be a mirage. (In Vietnam, the National Liberation Front and North Vietnam really were seeking to take over South Vietnam, and did so. In Iraq, by contrast, there really are no known weapons of mass destruction or known support for Al Qaeda.)

All this has by now been redundantly demonstrated, to the point of overfamiliarity, and public debate must shift to another subject: Will anyone be held accountable for the disaster (whose cost, still rising, remains beyond calculation)? Or has the past indeed been made "irrelevant," as Mr. Rapaille recommends? So far, the President appears to be following the Rapaille strategy.

He has adopted a practice of brushing aside the factual world with simple, declarative, false statements. For example, during his visit to Poland in late May, he declared, in defiance of all accepted information, "We've found the weapons of mass destruction." The statement, unsupported by evidence or even verbal backup from other Administration officials, was so strange it was widely uncommented upon. Everyone knows what to say if an official says something that later turns out to be false (for instance, that Saddam bought uranium in Africa). The suffix "-gate" is attached to it, and a process of sleuthing out the facts and tracing the origins of the falsehood ensues. But what are people to say or do or even think if the President states something that is already known by the whole world to be untrue? The problem arose again in the aftermath of the Kay report. The President had gone to war, he said, because Iraq possessed weapons of mass destruction. Kay was unable to find any. The President announced his vindication. Can black become white if the President says it is? Can the past be erased by White House fiat?

The Congressional supporters of the resolution have been wordier. Their evasions of accountability are too numerous to catalogue, but an interview that Democratic presidential candidate Senator John Kerry, who voted for the resolution but is now a keen critic of the President, gave to Tim Russert can suffice as an example of the genre. Kerry is angry. "Were you misled by the intelligence agencies?" Russert asked. "Were you duped?"

"No, we weren't. . . . The bottom line," he said, "is that we voted on the basis of information that was given to us that has since then been proven to be incorrect."

Then did he regret his vote for the resolution? If the information on which he voted for war was false, wasn't the vote a mistake—perhaps an understandable mistake but nevertheless a grievous one? By no means. "I don't wish I'd been a naysayer from the start. I did the right thing. My vote was a vote for the security of the United States of America based on the information we were given."

An example of a rare straight answer to the kind of question Russert was asking was given by Representative John Murtha, a conservative Democrat who voted for the resolution and now regrets it. "I am part of it. I admit the mistake," Murtha said. "We cannot allow these bureaucrats to get off when these young people [in Iraq] are paying such a price." He also said, "Somebody's got to be held responsible."

The most important actor in the story of the support for the war, however, is of course the voting public, which, according to polls, overwhelmingly supported the war when it was launched but now doubts the wisdom of its choice. Accountability, ultimately, rests in its hands. Will it hold the Administration responsible for the disaster? The answer may turn out to lie in two curious findings of polls conducted since the end of the conventional fighting. One was that, according to a Washington Post-ABC News poll in early April, 72 percent of the public thought the war would be worthwhile even if no biological or chemical weapons were found. The other was that, according to a recent *Washington Post* poll, 69 percent of the public believed it likely that Saddam Hussein was involved in planning or supporting the attacks of September 11.

Both beliefs are startling—the first because the Administration had tirelessly cited the Iraqi weapons threat as its chief reason for going to war, the second because there is no evidence of any involvement by Saddam in September 11. Many observers have criticized the White House for slyly and indirectly giving credence to the latter illusion, and criticized the press for failing to dispel it. There is justification for both criticisms, but deeper forces may be at work. Connecting the war on Iraq to September 11 has always been difficult work for the Administration. Many of its members had made no secret of their wish to overthrow Saddam Hussein long before the attack on American soil. (In 1998 neoconservative commentators William Kristol and Robert Kagan; Richard Perle, now a member of the Defense Policy Board; Elliott Abrams, now National Security Council Senior Director for Near East and North African Affairs; Richard Armitage, now Deputy Secretary of State; John Bolton, now Under Secretary of State; Donald Rumsfeld, now Defense Secretary; and Paul Wolfowitz, now Deputy Secretary of Defense, sent President Clinton a letter calling for the United States to attack and overthrow Saddam.)

The elaborate argumentation by which the Administration sought to present this preexisting wish as part of the post-9/11 "war on terror" has always been strained and difficult to follow as well as factually doubtful. Saddam seeks weapons of mass destruction—the argument ran—he supports terrorists; terrorists, too, want weapons of mass destruction; he may grant their wish; they may use them against the United States; therefore we must overthrow Saddam. Tenuous as this logic was, it had the political virtue of tying the war on Iraq to the 9/11 attacks.

A large part of the public, it appears, may have accepted the conclusion while overlooking the argumentation. That is, it may have seen the Iraq war as—somehow or other—a response to September 11 while never quite absorbing the allegation that provided the supposed link: the supposed Iraqi nuclear, biological, and chemical threat. After all, September 11—not the President's speeches thereafter—was the emotional and political earthshaker in the hearts and minds of the American people. The public's reactions in the future may therefore depend on whether it continues to associate September 11 with the war. But recent events, including the casualties suffered by US forces in Iraq, are tending to force the two apart in the public mind. The moment—will it be a year from now, when the presidential election is held?—that the public ceases to connect the attack and the war may well be the moment it holds the Administration accountable for the disaster it has brought to the United States and the world in Iraq.

Of all the responsibilities of government, the decision to go to war is the most grave. Can an Administration take the country to war on false pretexts and get away with it? A year ago, the issue was war and peace. Now the issue is the integrity of the American political system. Not democracy in Iraq or even the entire Middle East—that fading mirage—but democracy in the United States is now at stake.

Tautology in Action

NOVEMBER 17, 2003

A NEW JUSTIFICATION for our war on Iraq has been born out of the war itself. No one will have forgotten that the war was launched to remove weapons of mass destruction from Iraq (weapons that have turned out not to be there); to end support of Iraq for Al Qaeda (also missing); and to build a democracy in Iraq as a glowing lesson in governance for the whole Middle East (a democracy that looks more and more like a mirage). But now we are invited to set aside all these disproven or failing prewar justifications and embrace a new, postwar one: We must stay in Iraq because, having once gone in, we cannot afford to fail.

The claim has a certain argument-stopping plausibility. It seems to mark the boundaries of a new mainstream consensus. It has cross-appeal to war opposers and war supporters. War supporters are saved from having to confess error. In the Democratic primary contest alone there are four legislators—Dick Gephardt, John Kerry, John Edwards, and Joseph Lieberman—who voted for the Congressional resolution authorizing the war. All are now critical of the war, but not one has repented his vote.

All argue with the President over means only. They assert that the war is necessary, but he is fighting it in the wrong way. He must seek more foreign support; he must send in more American troops; he must recruit more Iraqi troops; he must come up with a better plan; he must give a better accounting for the $87 billion he has asked for; he must raise taxes in order to pay the sum. Everything about the war, they say, is wrong but the war itself, which remains right in spite of the collapse of all of its former justifications.

For some war opposers, too, the new justification is plausible, because it seems to acknowledge a responsibility toward the Iraqi people. Helping Iraq now becomes the cost to be paid for the mistake of going to war in the first place. And surely such an obligation does exist. Having removed the Iraqi state, the United States has incurred some kind of a duty to provide for the Iraqi people. The question, though, is: Provide what? If the United States were to restrict itself to supplying technical and humanitarian support, there could be no argument. The sooner Iraq's electricity is restored, its schools opened and its garbage picked up, the better. Probably, there is also a humanitarian argument for providing stop-gap security. Unfortunately, just this sort of expenditure is the least popular, as the vote in the Senate on the $87 billion demonstrated. Most senators had no problem voting the $67 billion to maintain our people in Iraq. It was the $20 billion earmarked for the Iraqi people that made Republicans and Democrats alike balk and seek to turn $10 billion of it into loans. In other words, these senators voted down the only part of the appropriation that would have directly satisfied an obligation to the Iraqi people. The result was an incoherent strategy: hugely funded American forces kept in Iraq to take care of themselves. They can take care of themselves better—and at lower cost— here in the United States.

What the United States chiefly proposes to provide for the Iraqi people is not in fact humanitarian aid. It proposes to provide them a democratic government. But a government is not like a sack of wheat. It cannot be unloaded from a ship with a USAID sticker on it. A government—if it is to be democratic—must proceed from the will of the governed. And with every day that passes it becomes clearer that the Iraqis do not wish to receive a new government from American hands. An unwanted gift is no gift at all, and it can never be an obligation to "give" one. A statement recently made by Ayatollah Ali Sistani, who probably represents mainstream Shiite opinion better than anyone else in Iraq, underscores this point. The occupying authority has decided to choose the framers of a new constitution for Iraq. However, Sistani says that Iraqis must choose the framers, in an election. The difference is fundamental. In the first case, the new order for Iraq originates in the occupying authority; in the second it originates in the Iraqi people. A constitution unmoored in the hearts of a people is no better than a "kite or balloon flying in the air," John Adams said. Goods and services are transferrable across national borders. Political will is not.

Nor for that matter is it at all clear that the United States wants what's best for the Iraqi people. George W. Bush has stated, "It's in the national interest of the United States that a peaceful Iraq emerge, and we will stay the course in order to achieve this objective." But the United States is not Iraq and what is good for it might well be a disaster for Iraq.

The new justification also has a strategic dimension that probably has greater weight with the decision-makers than any other consideration. Great powers hate to lose at anything. Once embarked on a course of action—even if it is a tragic mistake—they feel a compulsion to succeed that is not felt by smaller powers. Great powers' ambitions are far-flung, and if they fail in one place, they are more likely to be defied in another. They are as concerned for the reputation of their power as for its substance; indeed, the reputation is a good part of the substance. In the nineteenth century, the name for that reputation was "prestige." In the nuclear age, it became "credibility." The United States, for example, embarked upon the Vietnam War for many reasons. But the reason it refused to give up for more than a decade was to preserve the credibility of American power. Long after policymakers had concluded that no local stake was worth the continued cost, they still dared not lose the war for reasons of credibility. We cannot afford to lose, they said, as they now do today.

But the United States could lose and did lose. Costly as losing was, "winning"—indefinite occupation of the country—was discovered to be more costly still. Now once again, the logic of credibility threatens to introduce a fatal rigidity into policy. Policy becomes a tautology in action. We are there because we are there. We have to win because we cannot lose. Strategic retreat is ruled out. Yet nothing in this inflationary, self-reinforcing logic can change a jot of the situation on the ground, on which success or failure will ultimately depend. A policy that forsakes local reality for considerations of credibility is to geopolitics what a bubble is to economics. The bigger the bubble—superpowers beware!—the bigger the crash.

America's Vulnerable
Imperialism

November 24, 2003

In the wake of September 11, 2001, American political observers have adopted a surprising new piece of conventional wisdom: the United States has become an imperial power, and a global one at that. The old left-wing epithet "American imperialism" has become a term of approbation on the right and among many in the center. Exhibit A would be the overthrow of the Taliban government in Afghanistan, and exhibit B would be the occupation of Iraq. Beyond that new consensus, however, opinion has remained quite wildly divided. I count at least five radically diverging views.

One is that the United States, formerly only a republic, has now, without quite meaning to, also become an empire. Whether we like our new role or not, we have to get used to it. The writer Michael Ignatieff has expressed this view in the *The New York Times Magazine* and in his book *Empire Lite*, as has Robert Kaplan in his article "Supremacy by Stealth" in *The Atlantic*.

A second is that the United States cannot now become an empire, because it has been one for very a long time—at least since the Second World War, if not the whole twentieth century; and you cannot become what you already are. This is the view is of Noam Chomsky, but it is not confined to critics on the left. You can find it, for example, in *American Empire: The Realities and Consequences of U.S. Diplomacy*, by the former military officer Andrew J. Bacevich.

A third view is that the United States, the world's only super-power, is not yet quite an empire but should now frankly become one. It should spend the funds necessary to have its way in Iraq and throughout the Middle East. The hawkish columnist Charles Krauthammer and William Kristol, editor of the right-wing *Weekly Standard*, advance this view. They fault the administration for failing to summon means to match its ends.

A fourth view contends that, yes, the United States is already an empire, but we're botching the job—the British did it better. This is the theme of, among others, the British historian Niall Ferguson, in his book *Empire: the Rise and Demise of the British World Order and the Lessons for Global Power*.

Finally, there is the view that the United States was an empire for a long time, but now it is in decline, or is even collapsing. The heyday of American empire was in fact the immediate post-World-War-II period, after which its preeminence has faded. Charles Kupchan of the Brookings Institution develops this view in *The End of the American Era*, as does the scholar of empire Immanuel Wallerstein in his latest book *The Decline of American Power: The U.S. in a Chaotic World*.

The American empire seems, depending on whom you read,

to be expanding or collapsing, an old story or a new one, bestriding the world or melting away, staying the course or slinking toward the exit.

There are, of course, many kinds of empire and many definitions of empire. Some emphasize military strength, some economic exploitation, some cultural dominance. And yet whatever else empire may or may not be, it must, to deserve the name, include political dominance: the periphery must do what the center commands. Yet it is curiously just this aspect—the matter of political power—that the champions and builders of American empire appear to have scanted, or even overlooked entirely.

The administration's occupation policies in Iraq are an example. Certainly, The Bush administration's declared intention of democratizing the entire Middle East has the look of imperial political ambition. Yet at the same time, the administration has announced a likely reduction of American troop levels in Iraq. As in regard to the imperial project as a whole, we are left to wonder whether the United States is surrendering control or asserting it more firmly, pushing democracy or scuttling it, withdrawing or escalating, leaving or digging in, cutting and running or staying the course.

But the most astonishing instance of political neglect is the administration's omission before the war even to attempt to plan for the political future of Iraq. (The Pentagon in fact brushed aside the Future of Iraq plan that the State Department had drawn up.) The White House appears to have imagined that once the conventional battle against the ancien régime was won, its job was done, and a new state would build itself. When the president stood on the aircraft carrier under the made-in-the-White-House banner, "Mission Accomplished," he seems to have meant the military mission alone, and not to have conceived that military victory means little if it cannot be translated into political victory.

Historically, the political power of empires has depended on the creation of an indigenous force that both was prepared to carry out the commands of the imperial power and was grudgingly tolerated by its own people, whose acquiescence, however embittered, in the whole arrangement has always and everywhere been the sine qua non of imperial rule. But it was just this acquiescence that, in the course of the twentieth century, ran out in almost every country in the world, yielding to the resistance movements that were the main specific cause for the collapse of every single one of the great empires of the twentieth century, from the British to the Soviet. If the Iraqi people turn out to lack this rebellious sentiment—and so far there is no sign that they do—they will be one of the very few exceptions to the historical rule.

But has the administration, awakening belatedly to this central dilemma of the occupation, perhaps solved its political problem by deciding to immediately set up a provisional government? The new twist in policy is said to consist of "turning over" power to "the Iraqis," but it's not clear that the United States in fact yet possesses political power in Iraq or that the Iraqis in question—all American appointees—have or can acquire stature in their own country. For power, imperial or domestic, is not a fixed asset, like oil reserves, which can be turned over by one owner to another. In truth, the United States, for all its armed might, cannot really be said to exercise political power in Iraq, and it cannot hand over to someone else what it doesn't yet possess. If a provisional government is to wield power, it will have to build it from the ground up. But if and when it—or some other political grouping in Iraq—does really win power, it may no longer choose to take orders from the imperial center in Washington. In that case, the United States will have helped create the force that throws it out of Iraq.

The United States today is an unmatched military power. It is a great economic power. Yet politically—in Iraq and elsewhere—it is weak. And an empire with no political cement to hold it together is a sheet of loose sand. The consuls and proconsuls on the Potomac may have donned the imperial purple prematurely.

Is the United States, then, actually a global empire? Not quite yet. Can it become one? We'll see.

Kerry and War

MARCH 1, 2004

JOHN KERRY HAS been twice a hero. First, as a soldier in Vietnam, he displayed extraordinary physical courage, winning the Silver Star, the Bronze Star, and three Purple Hearts. Once, injured and under heavy fire, he turned back his riverboat to rescue a wounded comrade, who now credits Kerry with saving his life. Second, displaying civil courage at home equal to his physical courage in battle, he embarked on a campaign of protest against the war in which he had fought, becoming a spokesperson for Vietnam Veterans Against the War. In 1971, the VVAW camped out on the Mall in Washington. President Nixon's Justice Department then sought and obtained a court injunction forbidding the groups from using the Mall. Immediately and spontaneously, the veterans, as if reenacting the American Revolution, assembled in caucuses by state to deliberate and vote—and so created, at the symbolic center of the Republic, a kind of instant, ideal mini-republic of their own. They decided to defy the injunction and appeal their case to the Supreme Court, which reversed the lower court decision and permitted the protest to continue.

Kerry's subsequent words in testimony before the Senate Foreign Relations Committee on April 23, 1971, still have the power to startle, in our time of general disorientation and muted speech, with their brave candor. He described the wrong done to the Vietnam veterans but did not fail also to discuss the wrongs they had committed. "I would like," he said, "to talk on behalf of all those veterans and say that several months ago in Detroit we had an investigation at which over 150 honorably discharged, and many very highly decorated, veterans testified to war crimes committed in Southeast Asia. These were not isolated incidents but crimes committed on a day-to-day basis with the full awareness of officers at all levels of command. . . . They told stories that at times they had personally raped, cut off ears, cut off heads, taped wires from portable telephones to human genitals and turned up the power, cut off limbs, blown up bodies, randomly shot at civilians, razed villages in a fashion reminiscent of Genghis Khan, shot cattle and dogs for fun, poisoned food stocks and generally ravaged the countryside of South Vietnam in addition to the normal ravage of war and the normal and very particular ravaging which is done by the applied bombing power of this country." He added, "We call this investigation the Winter Soldier Investigation"—invoking Thomas Paine's description of the soldiers at Valley Forge. And he said, referring to the policy that had led to these crimes, "How do you ask a man to be the last man to die for a mistake?"

More than two decades later, Kerry made a decision that in the view of many observers failed to demonstrate the heroism of these earlier actions: On October 11, 2002, he voted, as did every other Democratic legislator with presidential ambitions but one—Representative Dennis Kucinich—to license George W. Bush to go to war against Iraq if he saw fit. Yet soon after the vote it turned out that the temper of the Democratic primary voters was antiwar, even angrily so, and Governor Howard Dean, who had opposed the war from the beginning, began his climb in the polls and became the generally acknowledged front-runner for the Democratic nomination. Kerry, previously considered the front-runner by many in the press, appeared to watch his longstanding presidential ambitions go down the drain. But then, in the Iowa caucuses and the New Hampshire primary, came the remarkable reversal of fortune in which Democratic voters, inspired by an almost palpable resolve to defeat Bush in the fall, switched their allegiance from the fiery Dean to the more phlegmatic and "electable" war hero Kerry, who soon won his long string of primary victories. In a peculiar act of political transplantation, the voters, energized by Dean, seemed by this switch to want to infuse the spirit of Dean into the body of Kerry, who then, Lazarus-like, came to life both as a person and as a candidate.

Left pending in all this maneuvering by ordinary citizens, however, was the question of Kerry's position on the war. Had our warrior-protester, now in pursuit of the presidency, sacrificed principle for ambition by voting for the Iraq war? Had the winter soldier abandoned his post? Had he by his vote asked American soldiers to die for a mistake? Only the Searcher of Hearts can know for sure. Kerry himself asserts that his vote to enable the war was a vote of conscience. What the rest of us can see, however, is that ever since his vote he has trapped himself in a morass—a little quagmire in its own right—of self-contradictory, equivocating, evasive, incomplete, unconvincing explanations of his stand.

Kerry has often said his position has been consistent, and this is true in the sense that he has said the same thing over and over. But it is in part precisely in this rigidity that the problem lies. Kerry voted for the war, he said at the time, because he believed that Saddam Hussein possessed weapons of mass destruction and must be disarmed. He favored "regime change" but did not regard it as a justification for war. He rejected the allegation of Iraqi ties with Al Qaeda as unproven. "Let me be clear," he said in his Senate speech announcing his vote for the war resolution. "The vote I will give the President is for one reason and one reason only: to disarm Iraq of weapons of mass destruction, if we cannot accomplish that objective through new, tough weapons inspections in joint concert with our allies." He lengthily detailed the intelligence findings he had seen, concluding, "These weapons represent an unacceptable threat." Disturbingly, he did not address the constitutional problem raised by the fact that, as his Massachusetts colleague Ted Kennedy said, "The most solemn responsibility any Congress has is the responsibility given the Congress by the Constitution to declare war." Therefore, "we would violate that responsibility if we delegate that responsibility to the President in advance before the President himself has decided the time has come for war."

The measure was the only substantive one that Kerry or any senator would pass before the war, yet Kerry claimed to believe that his vote was conditioned on fulfillment of "promises" that the Administration had made. The promises were to exhaust all diplomatic possibilities before going to war and thereby to assemble a large international coalition to fight the war and help run Iraq when the war was over. Indeed, so great was his faith in these promises that he would later claim of himself and his fellow Democrats, "Nobody on our side voted for the war." What did they vote for, then? "We needed the legitimate threat of [war] to get our inspectors into Iraq." Kerry voted, it seems, for inspectors, not war. He and all of us got war.

Kerry's entire argument against the Administration therefore is not that it waged a mistaken war but that it waged a necessary war in the wrong way. Several interviewers have pushed him hard to explain his position. In August Tim Russert, on *Meet the Press*, noted that he was accusing the President of having "misled" the country and commented that this did not sound like someone who supported the war. Kerry disagreed. "Wrong," he said. "I supported the notion that we must as a country hold Saddam Hussein accountable for what he was doing." Only the conduct of the war bothered him. "And so I'm running because I'm angry at the mismanagement of how we worked with our colleagues in the world and how we, in fact, have conducted the war."

Russert proceeded to the key question: "No regret over your vote?" To which Kerry, dodging the question, answered, "My regret is that the President of the United States didn't do what he had said he would do"—namely go to war only when diplomacy was exhausted and allies were on board.

"Were you misled by the intelligence agencies?" Russert asked shortly.

Kerry wavered: "No, we weren't—I don't know whether we were lied to. I don't know whether they had the most colossal intelligence failure in history."

Chris Matthews of *Hardball* tried again in October. "Were we right to go to Iraq?" he asked.

"Not the way the President did it," answered Kerry.

Matthews pushed: Some other way, then? Would Kerry have gone to war if France—the symbol of the recalcitrant international community—had agreed? Kerry retreated as usual into generalities: "I would do whatever is necessary to protect the security of the United States."

Missing in all these responses and others Kerry has given is the answer to a simple, fair, necessary question—the one Kerry answered so memorably in regard to the Vietnam War: Was the war in Iraq a mistake? Disarming Saddam had been Kerry's only reason for going to war. If Saddam had no weapons of mass destruction, then wasn't the war a mistake, and wasn't a vote to authorize it a mistake, and hadn't he made that mistake? And wouldn't American soldiers (now totaling more than 500) as well as Iraqis (in their uncounted thousands) be once again dying for a mistake?

But—I can hear some readers asking—why talk about the past? Why jeopardize the famous "electability" that Kerry (whether intending to or not) acquired by voting for the war and turn the likely Democratic candidate (now ahead of George Bush in certain polls) into an antiwar man, "another McGovern"? Those risks are real, but so is the gain. For one thing, the issue of the war will not disappear even if, as seems likely, Dean fails to win the nomination. On the contrary, it is likely to grow in importance as the absence of weapons of mass destruction sinks in with the public and disorder in Iraq mounts. The essence of democracy is accountability. Kerry knows it. Of the President, he has rightly said, "George Bush needs to take responsibility for his actions and set the record straight. That's the very least that Americans should be able to expect from the

President of the United States. Either he believed Saddam Hussein had chemical weapons—or he didn't. Americans need to be able to trust their President—and they deserve the truth."

They deserve accountability and truth from opposition candidates as well. Someone who is ducking responsibility for his own actions is hardly in a strong position to call someone else to account. The Kay report can even be seen as an opportunity for Kerry. Kerry made a terrible error when, credulously trusting the dubious intelligence proffered by an Administration even then obviously hell-bent on war, he voted to authorize that war, but his responsibility is nowhere near as great as that of the President. He might even discover a political dividend. If he were to state that had he known in October 2002 what he knows now about Iraq's weapons program he would not have voted for the resolution, he would immediately win the enthusiasm of the antiwar Democrats, whose passion and resolve, thanks in great measure to Howard Dean, has brought a fighting spirit to the Democratic Party. Nor should he entirely shift blame to the Administration for lying to him. He should hold himself accountable for his own mistake. We need the winter soldier, now more than ever, back at his post.

Epilogue:
The Empire Backfires

THE FIRST ANNIVERSARY of the American invasion of Iraq has arrived. By now, we were told by the Bush Administration before the war, the flower-throwing celebrations of our troops' arrival would have long ended; their numbers would have been reduced to the low tens of thousands, if not to zero; Iraq's large stores of weapons of mass destruction would have been found and dismantled; the institutions of democracy would be flourishing; Kurd and Shiite and Sunni would be working happily together in a federal system; the economy, now privatized, would be taking off; other peoples of the Middle East, thrilled and awed, so to speak, by the beautiful scenes in Iraq, would be dismantling their own tyrannical regimes. Instead, 549 American soldiers and uncounted thousands of Iraqis, military and civilian, have died; some $125 billion has been expended; no weapons of mass destruction have been found; the economy is a disaster; electricity and water are sometime things; America's former well-wishers, the Shiites, are impatient with the occupation; terrorist bombs are taking a heavy toll; and Iraq as a whole, far from being a model for anything, is a cautionary lesson in the folly of imperial rule in the twenty-first century. And yet all this is only part of the cost of the decision to invade and occupy Iraq. To weigh the full cost, one must look not just at the war itself but away from it, at the progress of the larger policy it served, at things that have been done elsewhere—some far from Iraq or deep in the past—and, perhaps above all, at things that have been left undone.

Nuclear Fingerprints

While American troops were dying in Baghdad and Falluja and Samarra, Buhary Syed Abu Tahir, a Sri Lankan businessman, was busy making centrifuge parts in Malaysia and selling them to Libya and Iran and possibly other countries. The centrifuges are used for producing bomb-grade uranium. Tahir's project was part of a network set up by Abdul Qadeer Khan, the "father" of the Pakistani atomic bomb. This particular father stole most of the makings of his nuclear offspring from companies in Europe, where he worked during the 1980s. In the 1990s, the thief became a middleman—a fence—immensely enriching himself in the process. In fairness to Khan, we should add that almost everyone who has been involved in developing atomic bombs since 1945 has been either a thief or a borrower. Stalin purloined a bomb design from the United States, courtesy of the German scientist Klaus Fuchs, who worked on the Manhattan Project. China got help from Russia until the Sino-Soviet split put an end to it. Pakistan got secret help from China in the early 1970s. And now it turns out that Khan, among many, many other Pakistanis, almost certainly including the highest members of the government, has been helping Libya, Iran, North Korea and probably others obtain the bomb. That's apparently how Chinese designs—some still in Chinese—were found in Libya when its quixotic leader, Muammar Qaddafi, recently agreed to surrender his country's nuclear program to the International Atomic Energy Agency (IAEA). The rest of the designs were in English.

Were Klaus Fuchs's fingerprints on them? Only figuratively, because they were "copies of copies of copies," an official said. But such is the nature of proliferation. It is mainly a transfer of information from one mind to another. Copying is all there is to it. Sometimes, a bit of hardware needs to be transferred, which is where Tahir came in. Indeed, at least seven countries are already known to have been involved in the Pakistani effort, which Mohamed ElBaradei, the head of the IAEA, called a "Wal-Mart" of nuclear technology and an American official called "one-stop shopping" for nuclear weapons. Khan even printed a brochure with his picture on it listing all the components of nuclear weapons that bomb-hungry customers could buy from him. "What Pakistan has done," the expert on nuclear proliferation George Perkovich, of the Carnegie Endowment for International Peace, has rightly said, "is the most threatening activity of proliferation in history. It's impossible to overstate how damaging this is."

Another word for this process of copying would be globalization. Proliferation is merely globalization of weapons of mass destruction. The kinship of the two is illustrated by other details of Tahir's story. The Sri Lankan first wanted to build his centrifuges in Turkey, but then decided that Malaysia had certain advantages. It had recently been seeking to make itself into a convenient place for Muslims from all over the world to do high-tech business. Controls were lax, as befits an export platform. "It's easy, quick, efficient. Do your business and disappear fast, in and out," Karim Raslan, a Malaysian columnist and social commentator, recently told Alan Sipress of the *Washington Post*. Probably that was why extreme Islamist organizations, including Al Qaeda operatives, had often chosen to meet there. Global terrorism is a kind of globalization, too. The linkup of such terrorism and the world market for nuclear weapons is a specter that haunts the world of the twenty-first century.

THE WAR AND ITS AIMS

But aren't we supposed to be talking about the Iraq war on this anniversary of its launch? We are, but wars have aims, and the declared aim of this one was to stop the proliferation of weapons of mass destruction. In his State of the Union address in January 2002, the President articulated the threat he would soon carry out in Iraq: "The United States of America will not permit the world's most dangerous regimes to threaten us with the world's most destructive weapons." Later, he said we didn't want the next warning to be "a mushroom cloud." Indeed, in testimony before the Senate Foreign Relations Committee, Secretary of State Colin Powell explicitly ruled out every other justification for the war. Asked about the other reasons, he said, "The President has not linked authority to go to war to any of those elements." When Senator John Kerry explained his vote for the resolution authorizing the war, he cited the Powell testimony. Thus not only Bush but also the man likely to be his

Democratic challenger in this year's election justified war solely in the name of nonproliferation.

Proliferation, however, is not, as the President seemed to think, just a rogue state or two seeking weapons of mass destruction; it is the entire half-century-long process of globalization that stretches from Klaus Fuchs's espionage to Tahir's nuclear arms bazaar and beyond. The war was a failure in its own terms because weapons of mass destruction were absent in Iraq; the war policy failed because they were present and spreading in Pakistan. For Bush's warning of a mushroom cloud over an American city, though false with respect to Iraq, was indisputably well-founded in regard to Pakistan's nuclear one-stop-shopping: The next warning stemming from this kind of failure could indeed be a mushroom cloud.

The questions that now cry out to be answered are, Why did the United States, standing in the midst of the Pakistani nuclear Wal-Mart, its shelves groaning with, among other things, centrifuge parts, uranium hexafluoride (supplied, we now know, to Libya) and helpful bomb-assembly manuals in a variety of languages, rush out of the premises to vainly ransack the empty warehouse of Iraq? What sort of nonproliferation policy could lead to actions like these? How did the Bush Administration, in the name of protecting the country from nuclear danger, wind up leaving it wide open to nuclear danger?

In answering these questions, it would be reassuring, in a way, to report that the basic facts were discovered only after the war, but the truth is otherwise. In the case of Iraq, it's now abundantly clear that some combination of deception, self-deception and outright fraud (the exact proportions of each are still under investigation) led to the manufacture of a gross and avoidable falsehood. In the months before the war, most of the governments of the world strenuously urged the United States not to go to war on the basis of the flimsy and unconvincing evidence it was offering. In the case of Pakistan, the question of how much the Administration knew before the war has scarcely been asked, yet we know that the most serious breach—the proliferation to North Korea—was reported and publicized before the war.

It's important to recall the chronology of the Korean aspect of Pakistan's proliferation. In January 2003 Seymour Hersh reported in *The New Yorker* that Pakistan had given North Korea extensive help with its nuclear program, including its launch of a uranium enrichment process. In return, North Korea was sending guided missiles to Pakistan. In June 2002, Hersh revealed, the CIA had sent the White House a report on these developments. On October 4, 2002, Assistant Secretary of State for East Asia and Pacific Affairs James Kelly confronted the North Koreans with the CIA information, and, according to Kelly, North Korea's First Vice Foreign Minister, Kang Suk Ju, startled him by responding, "Of course we have a nuclear program." (Since then, the North Koreans have unconvincingly denied the existence of the uranium enrichment program.)

Bush of course had already named the Pyongyang government as a member of the "axis of evil." It had long been the policy of the United States that nuclearization of North Korea was intolerable. However, the Administration said nothing of the North Korean events to the Congress or the public. North Korea, which now had openly embarked on nuclear armament, and was even threatening to use nuclear weapons, was more dangerous than Saddam's Iraq. Why tackle the lesser problem in Iraq, the members of Congress would have had to ask themselves, while ignoring the greater in North Korea? On October 10, a week after the Kelly visit, the House of Representatives passed the Iraq resolution, and the next day the Senate followed suit. Only five days later, on October 16, did Bush's National Security Adviser, Condoleezza Rice, reveal what was happening in North Korea.

In short, from June 2002, when the CIA delivered its report to the White House, until October 16—the period in which the nation's decision to go to war in Iraq was made—the Administration knowingly withheld the news about North Korea and its Pakistan connection from the public. Even after the vote, Secretary of State Colin Powell strangely insisted that the North Korean situation was "not a crisis" but only "a difficulty." Nevertheless, he extracted a pledge from Pakistan's president, Pervez Musharraf, that the nuclear technology shipments to North Korea would stop. (They did not.) In March, information was circulating that both Pakistan and North Korea were helping Iran to develop atomic weapons. (The North Korean and Iranian crises are of course still brewing.)

In sum, the glaring contradiction between the policy of "regime change" for already disarmed Iraq and regime-support for proliferating Pakistan was not a postwar discovery; it was fully visible before the war. *The Nation* enjoys no access to intelligence files, yet in an article arguing the case against the war, this author was able to comment that an "objective ranking of nuclear proliferators in order of menace" would put "Pakistan first," North Korea second, Iran third and Iraq only fourth — and to note the curiosity that "the Bush Administration ranks them, of course, in exactly the reverse order, placing Iraq, which it plans to attack, first, and Pakistan, which it befriends and coddles, nowhere on the list." Was nonproliferation, then, as irrelevant to the Administration's aims in Iraq as catching terrorists? Or was protecting the nation and the world against weapons of mass destruction merely deployed as a smokescreen to conceal other purposes? And if so, what were they?

A New Leviathan

The answers seem to lie in the larger architecture of the Bush foreign policy, or Bush Doctrine. Its aim, which many have properly called imperial, is to establish lasting American hegemony over the entire globe, and its ultimate means is to overthrow regimes of which the United States disapproves, pre-emptively if necessary. The Bush Doctrine indeed represents more than a revolution in American policy; if successful, it would amount to an overturn of the existing international order. In the new, imperial order, the United States would be first among nations, and force would be first among its means of domination. Other, weaker nations would be invited to take their place in shifting coalitions to support goals of America's choosing. The United States would be so strong, the President has suggested, that other countries would simply drop out of the business of military competition, "thereby making the destabilizing arms races of other eras pointless, and limiting rivalries to trade and other pursuits of peace." Much as, in the early modern period, when nation-states were being born, absolutist kings, the masters of overwhelming military force within their countries, in effect said, "There is now a new thing called a nation; a nation must be orderly; we kings, we sovereigns, will assert a monopoly over the use of force, and thus supply that order," so now the United States seemed to be saying, "There now is a thing called globalization; the global sphere must be orderly; we, the sole superpower, will monopolize force throughout the globe, and thus supply international order."

And so, even as the Bush Administration proclaimed US military superiority, it pulled the country out of the world's major peaceful initiatives to deal with global problems—withdrawing from the Kyoto Protocol to check global warming and from the International Criminal Court, and sabotaging a protocol that would have given teeth to the biological weapons convention. When the UN Security Council would not agree to American decisions on war and peace, it became "irrelevant"; when NATO allies balked, they became "old Europe." Admittedly, these existing international treaties and institutions were not a full-fledged cooperative system; rather, they were promising foundations for such a system. In any case, the Administration wanted none of it.

Richard Perle, who until recently served on the Pentagon's Defense Policy Board, seemed to speak for the Administration in an article he wrote for the *Guardian* the day after the Iraq war was launched. He wrote, "The chatterbox on the Hudson [sic] will continue to bleat. What will die is the fantasy of the UN as the foundation of a new world order. As we sift the debris, it will be important to preserve, the better to understand, the intellectual wreckage of the liberal conceit of safety through international law administered by international institutions."

In this larger plan to establish American hegemony, the Iraq war had an indispensable role. If the world was to be orderly, then proliferation must be stopped; if force was the solution to proliferation, then pre-emption was necessary (to avoid that mushroom cloud); if pre-emption was necessary, then regime change was necessary (so the offending government could never build the banned weapons again); and if all this was necessary, then Iraq was the one country in the world where it all could be demonstrated. Neither North Korea nor Iran offered an opportunity to teach these lessons—the first because it was capable of responding with a major war, even nuclear war, and the second because even the Administration could see that US invasion would be met with fierce popular resistance. It's thus no accident that the peril of weapons of mass destruction was the sole justification in the two legal documents by which the Administration sought to legitimize the war—HJ Resolution 114 and Security Council Resolution 1441. Nor is it an accident that the proliferation threat played the same role in the domestic political campaign for the war—by forging the supposed link between the "war on terror" and nuclear danger. In short, absent the new idea that proliferation was best stopped by pre-emptive use of force, the new American empire would have been unsalable, to the American people or to Congress. Iraq was the foundation stone of the bid for global empire.

The reliance on force over cooperation that was writ large in the imperial plan was also writ small in the occupation of Iraq. How else to understand the astonishing failure to make any preparation for the political, military, policing and even technical challenges that would face American forces? If a problem, large or small, had no military solution, this Administration seemed incapable of even seeing it. The United States was as blind to the politics of Iraq as it was to the politics of the world.

Thus we don't have to suppose that Bush officials were indifferent to the spectacular dangers that Khan's network posed to the safety of the United States and the world or that the Iraqi resistance would pose to American forces. We only have to suppose that they were simply unable to recognize facts they had failed to acknowledge in their overarching vision of a new imperial order. In both cases, ideology trumped reality.

The same pattern is manifest on an even larger scale. Just now, the peoples of the world have embarked, some willingly and some not, on an arduous, wrenching, perilous, mind-exhaustingly complicated process of learning how to live as one indivisibly connected species on our one small, endangered planet. Seen in a certain light, the Administration's imperial bid, if successful, would amount to a kind of planetary coup d'état, in which the world's dominant power takes charge of this process by virtue of its almost freakishly superior military strength. Seen in another, less dramatic light, the American imperial solution has interposed a huge, unnecessary roadblock between the world and the Himalayan mountain range of urgent tasks that it must accomplish no matter who is in charge: saving the planet from overheating; inventing a humane, just, orderly, democratic, accountable global economy; redressing mounting global inequality and poverty; responding to human rights emergencies, including genocide; and, of course, stopping proliferation as well as rolling back the existing arsenals of nuclear arms. None of these exigencies can be met as long as the world and its greatest power are engaged in a wrestling match over how to proceed.

Does the world want to indict and prosecute crimes against humanity? First, it must decide whether the International Criminal Court will do the job or entrust it to unprosecutable American forces. Do we want to reverse global warming and head off the extinction of the one-third of the world's species that, according to a report published in Nature magazine, are at risk in the next fifty years? First, the world's largest polluter has to be drawn into the global talks. Do we want to save the world from weapons of mass destruction? First, we have to decide whether we want to do it together peacefully or permit the world's only superpower to attempt it by force of arms.

No wonder, then, that the Administration, as reported by Robert F. Kennedy Jr., has mounted an assault on the scientific findings that confirm these dangers to the world. The United States' destructive hyperactivity in Iraq cannot be disentangled from its neglect of global warming. Here, too, ideology is the enemy of fact, and empire is the nemesis of progress.

If the engine of a train suddenly goes off the rails, a wreck ensues. Such is the war in Iraq, now one year old. At the same time, the train's journey forward is canceled. Such is the current paralysis of the international community. Only when the engine is back on the tracks and starts in the right direction can either disaster be overcome. Only then will everyone be able to even begin the return to the world's unfinished business.

APPENDIX

End the Nuclear Danger:
An Urgent Call

BY JONATHAN SCHELL, RANDALL CAROLINE FORSBERG
& DAVID CORTRIGHT

A DECADE after the end of the cold war, the peril of nuclear
destruction is mounting. The great powers have refused to give
up nuclear arms, other countries are producing them and terrorist
groups are trying to acquire them.

POORLY GUARDED warheads and nuclear material in the
former Soviet Union may fall into the hands of terrorists. The
Bush Administration is developing nuclear "bunker busters" and
threatening to use them against nonnuclear countries. The risk of
nuclear war between India and Pakistan is grave.

DESPITE THE END of the cold war, the United States plans to
keep large numbers of nuclear weapons indefinitely. The latest
US-Russian treaty, which will cut deployed strategic warheads to
2,200, leaves both nations facing "assured destruction" and lets
them keep total arsenals (active and inactive, strategic and tactical)
of more than 10,000 warheads each.

THE DANGERS POSED by huge arsenals, threats of use, proliferation and terrorism are linked: The nuclear powers' refusal to
disarm fuels proliferation, and proliferation makes nuclear materials more accessible to terrorists.

THE EVENTS of September 11 brought home to Americans what it means to experience a catastrophic attack. Yet the horrifying losses that day were only a fraction of what any nation would suffer if a single nuclear weapon were used on a city.

THE DRIFT TOWARD catastrophe must be reversed. Safety from nuclear destruction must be our goal. We can reach it only by reducing and then eliminating nuclear arms under binding agreements.

WE THEREFORE CALL ON THE UNITED STATES AND RUSSIA TO FULFILL THEIR COMMITMENTS UNDER THE NONPROLIFERATION TREATY TO MOVE TOGETHER WITH THE OTHER NUCLEAR POWERS, STEP BY CAREFULLY INSPECTED AND VERIFIED STEP, TO THE ABOLITION OF NUCLEAR WEAPONS. AS KEY STEPS TOWARD THIS GOAL, WE CALL ON THE UNITED STATES TO:

§ RENOUNCE the first use of nuclear weapons.

§ Permanently END the development, testing and production of nuclear warheads.

§ SEEK AGREEMENT with Russia on the mutual and verified destruction of nuclear weapons withdrawn under treaties, and increase the resources available here and in the former Soviet Union to secure nuclear warheads and material and to implement destruction.

§ STRENGTHEN nonproliferation efforts by ratifying the Comprehensive Test Ban Treaty, finalizing a missile ban in

North Korea, supporting UN inspections in Iraq, locating and reducing fissile material worldwide and negotiating a ban on its production.

§ TAKE nuclear weapons off hairtrigger alert in concert with the other nuclear powers (the UK, France, Russia, China, India, Pakistan and Israel) in order to reduce the risk of accidental or unauthorized use.

§ INITIATE talks on further nuclear cuts, beginning with US and Russian reductions to 1,000 warheads each.

TO SIGN THE STATEMENT, GO TO *URGENTCALL.ORG* OR SEND NAME, ORGANIZATION/PROFESSION (FOR ID ONLY) AND CONTACT INFORMATION TO URGENT CALL, c/o FOURTH FREEDOM FORUM, 11 DUPONT CIRCLE NW, 9TH FLOOR, WASHINGTON, DC 20036. WE NEED TAX-DEDUCTIBLE DONATIONS, MADE TO URGENT CALL, TO DISSEMINATE THIS CALL. PLEASE MAIL TO THE SAME ADDRESS.

THIS CALL WAS DRAFTED BY JONATHAN SCHELL, THE HAROLD WILLENS PEACE FELLOW OF THE NATION INSTITUTE AND THE AUTHOR OF *THE FATE OF THE EARTH*; RANDALL CAROLINE (RANDY) FORSBERG, DIRECTOR OF THE INSTITUTE FOR DEFENSE AND DISARMAMENT STUDIES AND AUTHOR OF THE "CALL TO HALT THE NUCLEAR ARMS RACE," THE MANIFESTO OF THE 1980s NUCLEAR WEAPONS FREEZE CAMPAIGN; AND DAVID CORTRIGHT, PRESIDENT OF THE FOURTH FREEDOM FORUM AND FORMER EXECUTIVE DIRECTOR OF SANE.

Acknowledgments

THE WRITING OF the series of articles assembled in this book was made possible by The Nation Institute, where I am the Harold Willens Peace Fellow; *The Nation* magazine, where almost all of the articles were published; and, of course, Nation Books, which has put the articles between these covers. At The Nation Institute, I want to thank—in addition to Hamilton Fish, the Institute's president, to whom this book is dedicated—Taya Grobow, Janine Jaquet, and Wylia Sims, who make life not only functional but agreeable. At *The Nation* magazine, I want to thank the magazine's editor Katrina vanden Heuvel, who invited me to write the "Letter from Ground Zero" series and gave steady support and always helpful and invaluable advice; Karen Rothmyer, kind, careful, and thoughtful editor; and Roane Carey, meticulous reader. At Nation books, I want to thank Carl Bromley, whose idea it was to publish the series as a book, and Ruth Baldwin, skilled and tactful shepherd of the project to completion. I want also to thank Nayan Chanda, editor of Yaleglobal Online, who suggested and first published the two articles "Politics in Command" and "America's Vulnerable Imperialism."